All About
Siamese Cats
TS-129

t.f.h.

Title page: Siamese cats have a body of one color and "points" (tail, feet, ears, and face) of another color. The color of the points distinguishes the varieties of the breed and gives them their names. Owner, Norma Volpe.

Photography: Mike Anderson, Brenda Conner, Jim Cooper, Donna Coss, Fred Fischer, Isabelle Francais, Dorothy Holby, Jane Howard, Dolores and William Kennedy, Dr. Robert C. Koestler, Trisha McKenney, Miceli Studios, Ltd., Roger Michael, Horst Müller, Fritz Prenzel, Ron Reagan, Lynn Y. Sakai, Stephen Sakai, Skotzke & Lucas, Don Stemple, Terry Stracke, Sally Anne Thompson, Eloise I. Trosan, Frank Wimmer.

Drawings: John R. Quinn.

Dedicated to Sandy Tan for her advice and support.

Distributed in the UNITED STATES by T.F.H. Publications, Inc., One T.F.H. Plaza, Neptune City, NJ 07753; in CANADA to the Pet Trade by H & L Pet Supplies Inc., 27 Kingston Crescent, Kitchener, Ontario N2B 2T6; Rolf C. Hagen Ltd., 3225 Sartelon Street, Montreal 382 Quebec; in CANADA to the Book Trade by Macmillan of Canada (A Division of Canada Publishing Corporation), 164 Commander Boulevard, Agincourt, Ontario M1S 3C7; in ENGLAND by T.F.H. Publications, PO Box 15, Waterlooville PO7 6BQ; in AUSTRALIA AND THE SOUTH PACIFIC by T.F.H. (Australia) Pty. Ltd., Box 149, Brookvale 2100 N.S.W., Australia; in NEW ZEALAND by Ross Haines & Son, Ltd., 82 D Elizabeth Knox Place, Panmure, Auckland, New Zealand; in the PHILIPPINES by Bio-Research, 5 Lippay Street, San Lorenzo Village, Makati, Rizal; in SOUTH AFRICA by Multipet Pty. Ltd., P.O. Box 35347, Northway, 4065, South Africa. Published by T.F.H. Publications, Inc. Manufactured in the United States of America by T.F.H. Publications, Inc.

ALL ABOUT
SIAMESE CATS

BARBARA S. BURNS

Gr. Ch.
Serendipity
Casia of Tosa,
a female Lilac
Point. Owner,
Sandy Tan.

Contents

CHAPTER

1

What Makes the Siamese Special?

THEIR ROYAL BACKGROUND

Although the exact origin of the Siamese cat can't be proved, all probable theories suggest that it was a sacred cat, related perhaps to the temple cat of Burma or the sacred cat of ancient Egypt. The close resemblance of the Siamese to statues of Bast, the cat goddess of Egypt, reinforces this possibility. The slanted deep blue eyes of the Siamese, as well as its distinctive color markings, known as points, have attracted admiration and adulation over the centuries.

Written records verify that Siamese cats were royal pets and temple guards as early as the 1600s in Siam, now Thailand. So highly were they regarded that their ownership is said to have been restricted to members of the royal family. Only if a man was promoted to a knight or nobleman could he possess that cat with, as they believed, "special powers." Ancient texts said that not only was the body of the Siamese unique, but the eye color was like none other. "Their eyes resembled the eye color of the European . . . blue."

Delightful legends abound to explain the occasional cross-eyed or kink-tailed Siamese. Incidentally, although these characteristics are sought by an occasional pet buyer, they are avoided by Siamese breeders who wish to show their cats. A visible kink or crossed eyes are both cause for disqualification in the show ring. Actually, a kink that can be felt, even though it isn't visible, often tends to make a judge avoid giving the cat a win.

The earlier cats were also

The Siamese has a unique, distinctive appearance. This is Ch. (CFA) and Gr. Ch. (ACFA) Caru Chizu Adamma, a Chocolate Point owned by Dayle Russell.

heavier-bodied and what we call "apple-headed" today. That is, they didn't have the long, svelte look so sought after in the show ring. The contemporary Siamese is long-headed, long-eared, long-bodied, long-legged, and long-tailed. Some people who owned the Siamese of 20 years ago resent these changes, but there is little question that today's Siamese is extremely refined and striking in appearance.

LEGENDS ABOUT THEIR HERITAGE

One of the stories which accounts for the cross-eyed or kink-tailed Siamese recounts a time in Siam when all of the men went off

This pensive Seal Point is Calkin's Free Spirit of Tohpao, owned by Brenda Conner.

to defend their kingdom, leaving only a male and female Siamese to guard the golden goblet, once used by Buddha, in the sacred temple. The male Siamese, being a tom cat and having already impregnated the female, became restless and went off seeking other pretty females. The faithful queen (as females are called) became so concerned over the vastness of her responsibility to guard the goblet that she not only stared at it with concentrated eyes but also wrapped her long and lovely tail around it in case she should cat nap.

As time passed and her kittening time came closer and closer, she increased her vigilance, hoping that some of the monks would return. At last she could wait no longer—sixty-eight days had passed, probably the longest gestation for any feline breed (but not unusual for a Siamese, even today), and her lovely babies were born—but, alas, all with crossed eyes as hers had become from watching the goblet, and all with kink tails as hers had become from being wrapped about the goblet.

Those kink tails and crossed eyes do show up occasionally to this day, reinforcing this legend and other similar ones. The kink tails certainly do no harm to the health of the cat, but badly crossed eyes can affect the vision adversely.

THEIR IMPORTATION TO GREAT BRITAIN AND THE UNITED STATES

From the time the first Siamese were imported to Great Britain in the 1880s, the breed became a great favorite. It is believed that the first pair, Pho and Mia, were brought by Owen Gould, the Consul General in Bangkok, and later shown at the Crystal Palace Exhibition in 1886.

It is said that President Rutherford B. Hayes received the first Siamese cat ever sent to the United States and that it became a great White House celebrity. In any event, Siamese had their first public showing in the United States in 1903 and gained immediate acceptance.

CHARACTERISTICS OF THE SIAMESE

The uniqueness of the Siamese lies not only in its appearance, but in its affectionate, sociable nature. Many people compare the Siamese personality to that of a dog. These cats are more concerned with pleasing their owners than are cats of other breeds, and, for this reason, are easier to train.

Anyone who has ever owned a Siamese (or been owned by a Siamese) can tell you that this cat is very talkative and soon teaches you what the different meows indicate—*demand* might be a better word. There is the meow that says to get up in the morning, the meow for mealtime, the meow to get the company out of his favorite chair (and, in fact, to get rid of the

Ch. Eldamar's Mirage of Tohpao, known as "Lady" to her human family, and her four-month-old kitten. Interaction with its mother is important to a kitten's development.

They enjoy being on your lap, held in your arms, snuggled up next to you on a chair or couch, and, if you'll let them, sharing your bed.

Siamese really don't thrive without the company of man. They may enjoy another cat, especially if they are left alone most of the day, but their real love is for their owner or owners. Their craving for the love of humans seems to be a breed characteristic.

company unless, of course, the company is finding the cat irresistible), the voice of the un-neutered male, and, worst of all, the female in season. Your neighbors or friends on the other end of the telephone will swear a baby is crying.

Because they are so intelligent, Siamese are forever curious about anything or anyone who comes into the house. They'll go through your grocery bags in a hurry if you aren't careful. They seem to know if you brought goodies or food for them. They're also mischievous and will entertain you with their antics by the hour, especially if you have a pair.

PERSONALITIES OF THE FOUR COLORS

Four colors of the Siamese are recognized by the Cat Fanciers' Association (CFA), the largest cat registry group in the United States.

A Blue Point Siamese. The ears of a Siamese should be strikingly large.

Fortunately their more boisterous fun and games can be controlled with careful early training. For example, they won't climb the drapes or ruin your furniture if they're provided with a scratching post and if you keep their claws clipped.

Many Siamese enjoy riding in a car, and they can be trained to walk on a leash. They love to fetch a paper ball or small toy, jump from the floor to your arms, sit up, bow, and maybe even play a brisk game of hide-and-seek. Mainly they just plain enjoy you as their owner and friend.

They are the Seal Point, the Chocolate Point, the Blue Point, and the Lilac Point. Although some other associations recognize the Red Point, the Cream Point, and various Lynx and Tortie Points as being within the Siamese class, CFA lists them as a separate breed, known as Colorpoints. Most of the national Siamese breed clubs support the theory that only these four colors—Seal, Chocolate, Blue, and Lilac—are true Siamese. The others are regarded as hybrids. Reds, for example, do not breed true and tend to be larger than the other colors, being

The striking contrast between the color of the points and body adds to the appeal of members of this breed. This is La Vond's Gr. Pr. Ramachandra, a Seal Point neuter owned by La Vond Thompson.

a cross between the American Shorthair and the Siamese.

Over the years, the Seal Point, the earliest Siamese described, has continued to be a great favorite with the public, but more and more, the other three colors are gaining acceptance in the show ring and as pets. Interestingly, the four colors not only look different from each other but seem to have somewhat different personalities. Naturally there are exceptions, since the personality of the mother cat as well as early handling and training are also very significant factors in molding the traits of a kitten.

Seal Points: The body color should be a pale fawn with the points a dense, deep seal brown, almost black. (The points include the facial mask, ears, legs, feet, and tail. The Thais also included the genitals and probably rightly so.) The Seal Points tend to darken with age, especially the females that are bred. Young Seals are very flashy and elegant, and they seem to know it. They are more dignified than the other colors. They also tend to be possessive of their owners and to dislike change in their environment. Some Seals may not like being held, handled, or groomed as much as the other colors.

This cat is a Tonkinese, known familiarly to some fanciers as a "Tonk." Tonks were created by crossing Siamese with Burmese.

They prefer to come to you, not you to them.

Chocolate Points: These are the dilutes of the Seal Points, that is, the lighter version. The points are the color of milk chocolate, and the body is ivory and tends to stay light. Sometimes their points may not be as complete as those of the Seals. A really outstanding "Choc" may have a cinnamon hue. They are wonderful pets since they are the clowns of the breed and enjoy entertaining you. They are also extremely affectionate and love to kiss and nibble ears. They are probably the most extroverted of the four colors. They want to have fun and will go along with almost anything. In the past, they've tended to be less refined in bone structure than the other colors (being the last perfected), but, in

the past few years, they have become increasingly svelte and successful in the show ring.

Blue Points: Blues come in two shades, a deep slate blue and a lighter silver blue, both acceptable in the show ring. Their bodies should be a pale gray blue, not beige. As with Seals, they may darken with age. Most breeders would agree that they are the most loyal to their owners and extremely affectionate. They will purr just because you meet their eyes. Some will hold your gaze as long as possible, as with the "meditation cats" in ancient writings. They love to jump on your shoulder and be carried around. Probably they care the most about being physically close to their owners. They'll purr most of the night if allowed to sleep with you. They're seldom aggressive with other cats.

Lilac Points: These are the dilutes of the Blue Points. They are known as Frost Points in some U.S. associations and in Great Britain. Their points are a pale pinkish lilac and their bodies, glacial white. They tend to stay light all of their lives. Although not as flashy as the Seals, they have a subtle beauty all their own. Some people compare the females to Jean Harlow. Both the females and males often have what might be called artistic temperaments. At times they are melodramatic—for example, if they don't get their way or their special treat you promised them. They seem to believe and expect you to believe that they are truly superior in beauty and intelligence. Often in a household with other cats they become the instigators of assorted pranks based on "getting our way." They do demand your attention and are very slick at getting it.

"KISSIN' COUSINS"

Because of their unique color pattern, vivid blue eyes, svelte Oriental bodies, outgoing personalities, and impressive intelligence, Siamese cats have been utilized to create many new breeds. Some of these "kissin' cousins" bear a

strong family resemblance; others don't look as obviously related.

Included in the list of offspring breeds are the Balinese, Burmese, Colorpoint Shorthair, Foreign Shorthairs, Havana Brown, Himalayan, Javanese, Manxamese, Ocicat, and the Tonkinese. There are others which might be listed, but some of their breeders insist they arose spontaneously.

Those most similar are what CFA calls Colorpoint

The Havana Brown, which originated in Great Britain, was created by crossing a Seal Point Siamese carrying the chocolate color and a shorthaired black.

Shorthairs, including all the colors of pointed Siamese-type cats other than the classic seal, blue, chocolate, and lilac. Among these are the red and cream points and the lynx or tabby (striped) points occurring in all possible colors, the tortie (spotted) points in all possible colors, and the combination tabby-tortie points in all different colors. Some registry associations

The Siamese cat is noted for its highly intelligent and alert nature.

in the U.S. and Europe combine all of these under the Siamese category, but, genetically, this seems to have its drawbacks since the interbreeding of all the colors results in less clear color for all of them. A controversy beyond the scope of this book is involved.

Another somewhat controversial cat is the albino Siamese, not really a separate color but a cat with a pigmentation deficiency. The albino is white with pink skin and a pink undertone to the pale blue eyes.

The unique coat color pattern of the Siamese is the result of a recessive, albinistic mutation, which prevents full pigmentation from appearing anywhere but at the extremities or points. This mutation also occurs in rabbits and cavies. These animals are all affected by temperature, the points being the coldest part of the body. This coat pattern is known as the "Himalayan."

That's why the pointed Siamese-Persian cross is called the Himalayan. It has the pattern of the Siamese and its blue eyes (though not as dark) and the long hair and more massive body of the Persian. Since both the colorpoint pattern and the longhair genes are recessive, the creation of the highly popular "Himmy" is a real genetic triumph. It is known as the Colorpoint Longhair in Europe.

The beautiful Balinese is simply a longhaired Siamese, recognized by CFA in the four basic colors of the Siamese, with the Javanese being the Colorpoint Shorthair counterpart, occurring in all its color possibilities. Some associations call these cats Oriental Longhairs because they retain the Oriental body of the Siamese.

Ragdolls and Birmans also display the Siamese color pattern, though their origins are controversial.

The Tonkinese, created by crossing the Siamese and the Burmese (which was created some years earlier through the use of the Siamese), also retains the Siamese points, but the contrast between body color and points is less striking, and the eyes are aqua, not blue. The "Tonks," as they are known familiarly, come in five colors: natural mink, champagne mink, blue mink, honey mink, and

Another Siamese "cousin" is the Burmese. Note the rich color and texture of the coat of this adult female.

platinum mink, the term "mink" being a reference to the silky texture of the coat. This breed is ideally a happy medium between the rather cobby-bodied Burmese and the slender, lithe Siamese. Admirers of the old style "apple-headed" Siamese often find the Tonkinese appealing in its similarity to these earlier cats. If anything, they are even friendlier and more outgoing than the Siamese.

Other exciting offshoots of the Siamese are solid color "cousins," usually with Oriental body type. Their development began in Great Britain with the crossing of the Russian Blue and the Siamese to create the Foreign Lavender, and the crossing of the Russian Blue, assorted Shorthairs, and the Siamese to create the Chestnut Brown, known as the Havana Brown in the U.S.

Generally, the term "foreign" is used in Great Britain to designate all the shorthaired varieties other

The highly popular Himalayan, or "Himmy," is the result of a Siamese-Persian cross.

than the British Shorthair. The cats labelled "foreign," including the black and white as well as the lavender, have the Siamese body type, whereas the British Shorthairs are chunkier.

The Havana Brown is a rich tobacco brown, from which its name has come. Its deep green eyes and brown whiskers, which match its coat, make the breed very distinctive. This cousin bears less family resemblance than most of the others because of its solid color and cobbier body.

Once the self-colored (solid) cats were created in Great Britain, the cat fancy in the U.S. became interested in the development of a Siamese-type cat without points, which would basically

Some cat organizations recognize only the Seal Point, Chocolate Point, Lilac Point, and Blue Point as true Siamese and classify cats with point colors other than these as a separate breed (Colorpoint Shorthair).

A Siamese lends an air of grace and refinement to any home.

conform to the same judging standard as that of the Siamese (except for color). American Shorthairs were crossed with Siamese to create the Oriental Shorthair. They now come in a wide variety of solid, shaded, parti, and exotic tabby patterns. Some look like small jungle cats. Their eyes are green except those of the solid whites, which may be blue. Today's Oriental Shorthairs are backcrossed to the Siamese or Colorpoint Shorthair every few generations to retain body type, but the American Shorthair is no longer involved in the breeding.

The most recent manmade breed related to the Siamese is the glamorous Ocicat, which looks as if it came straight from the jungle but doesn't carry any wild blood. A spotted cat, very exotic and feral in appearance, the "Oci" has the intelligence and gentle temperament of the Siamese. It was created by Virginia Daly of Dalai Cattery in Berkeley, Michigan, by crossing the Siamese, Abyssinian, and American Shorthair. One of the fastest-growing registries in all of the associations, the Oci is extremely popular, and new breeders are appearing all over. Since their acceptance by CFA (Provisional in 1986), Ocicats have been limited to outcrosses with Abyssinians only, and this outcross will be permitted only until 1995, after which time the breed must stand on its own. Ocis come in a range of colors with the most popular being the brown or black spotted on a ruddy background and the black spotted on a silver background. This new breed is already a big winner in the show ring, as well as in public acceptance.

Those ubiquitous Siamese certainly have been generous about sharing their unique color pattern, body style, and personality to create pleasing new breeds! We may call them manmade, but who knows what the Siamese might call them if they could speak— other than, of course, "kissin' cousins" or, in some instances, "hissin' cousins."

This stunning Siamese "cousin" is an Ocicat. This breed was created by crossing the Siamese, the Abyssinian, and the American Shorthair. Ocis are favored by some fanciers because of their exotic appearance, as well as their even temperament.

CHAPTER 2

Buying Your Siamese Kitten

DECIDING WHAT YOU WANT

Once you've fallen in love with the Siamese breed and decided you must have a kitten, your search begins. Actually it shouldn't be difficult to find the kitten you want if you have some idea of where and how to look. It is quite natural that most people think of their local pet shop as a source for purchasing a kitten; remember, however, that a pet shop cannot possibly stock a large selection of Siamese kittens at all times. If, by chance, your pet shop does not carry the type of cat you desire, you might consider contacting a breeder, who may have the particular cat that you are seeking. A veterinarian you've known and taken your pets to may very well be able to suggest breeders in your area who might have Siamese kits for sale.

Sometimes, exhibitors at cat shows will have kittens for sale. The various cat publications are another source of information that you might want to look into. Relatively new is the use of computer referral services that provide listings of breeders.

It will be helpful if you have as clear an idea as possible of what you're looking for. That is, do you want a pet to love and to cherish for the next 15 to 20 years? The best show cat you can find? Or something somewhere in between, sometimes called a "breeder?" Would you be willing to pay more for your pet because you want an outstanding representative of the breed? Is the pedigree important to you? These questions should be answered before you select a kitten.

"It will be helpful if you have as clear an idea as possible of what you're looking for."

This cute Siamese kit is Miyo Mid-Nite Express of Saroko, a Seal Point male owned by Dr. Robert C. Koestler.

A profile study of Gr. Ch. Sin-Chiang Brandie of De Vegas, a Seal Point female owned by Dan and Hanne Gauger.

Inflation seems to have taken its toll on the cat market as well as most others. A top show kitten is difficult to find because most breeders want to keep their very best or sell them out of area. The reason for this is that they don't want to compete against their own cattery weekend after weekend. Also, as a newcomer, you may find that some breeders tend to be a little wary of you. Some may already have waiting lists for their very top cats. Some would rather wait and see how you work out as a potential exhibitor and, possibly, breeder. After all, a breeder has only so many top cats per year, and even if you're willing to pay a top price, you may not be experienced enough to show the cat to its highest potential. In fact, breeders who are anxious to sell a so-called top show cat might not be your best resource—not unless you find out all you can about them.

WHY NOT JUST A PET?

If what you want is a house pet to love and be loved by, then you should shop for a pet kitten and make that clear to the seller. If you really care—for vanity's sake—about a pedigree, you can probably obtain it after you provide proof that you have had your cat neutered. If the breeder has provided a registration slip, he will have marked it "Not To Be Bred." The pedigree isn't important at all unless your cat is to be bred, nor is the registration. What's important is that you and your pet are happy.

WHY NOT BREED MY CAT AT LEAST ONCE?

There's an old saw that says a female cat will be happier and healthier if she has been bred at least once. This really isn't true. In fact, if you plan to keep your female as a pet, it's better that you have her spayed before she starts coming into season. Otherwise she'll be more interested in her estrus cycle than her happy life as a pet. Finding a compatible male, paying the stud fee, and helping to raise the kittens may be more work than fun. In any event, going through this probably isn't worth it if the main thing you wanted was to provide a companion cat—a son or daughter—for your original cat. Many breeders will give you a break in price if you take two kittens at once, related or unrelated, so that they can be companion cats. They know the kittens will probably be happier. This, in most instances, might be the simplest way to go.

Another problem for the inexperienced breeder is selling and placing the other kittens, especially if you've paid a stud fee and hope to come out even or realize a profit. The shortest ad in a major Sunday newspaper can be costly, as can ads in national cat magazines. A free ad on a food market bulletin board will bring you little or nothing unless the potential customer thinks the kittens are free or very minimally priced.

For all of these reasons, you should probably have your female spayed at approximately nine months. Some come into season even earlier and should be spayed as soon as the season ends. Spaying during a season usually

Who could resist as lovely a "present" as this? This ten-month-old already displays the remarkable charm of the Siamese breed.

Like members of other breeds of cat, young Siamese enjoy the warmth and security of their littermates. Brenda Conner, owner.

costs more because it's more of a problem for the veterinarian and the cat.

BACKYARD BREEDERS

Reputable breeders are very much opposed to those who are sometimes referred to as "backyard breeders." These are people who breed their females with the hope of making money and have no real interest in upgrading the breed and little or no concern for the health of the mother and kittens. The kittens are sold cheap but are often infested with fleas, ear mites, worms, etc., and may have runny eyes and noses. They are usually very poor specimens of the breed. Sometimes these same breeders offer stud service at a low price. But beware! If you buy a sickly kitten and fall in love with it, you may spend more in the end than you would have spent on a lovely, healthy

specimen of the breed.

If you go to buy your first kitten from a reputable cattery and the breeder gets the impression that you aren't certain about whether you want a pet or whether you may be a future backyard breeder, he'll probably be less than cordial. If you want a pet to love and cherish, say so. If you think you may be interested in a cat to breed or show, say so. The prices go up, naturally. But so does the quality of the kitten. What no one wants is for you to buy a so-called pet without papers and then end up breeding it over and over and selling the kittens cheap, i.e., becoming a backyard breeder.

BUYING THE PAPERS

It's possible that a breeder may have for sale a kitten that is potentially a breeder or even a show cat, though not necessarily a top show cat, which he will sell for a lesser amount without the pedigree (papers) but for which he asks more if you want the registration and pedigree. In this case, you have a decision to make—if you haven't already made your decision about what you want. If you're certain you want only a pet, most breeders will give you the registration slip marked "Not To Be Bred" and probably offer the papers after the cat has been neutered.

If the kitten does develop into a beauty and you have the papers, then you can register it with CFA or whatever association it has been registered in and show it or breed it. Without a pedigree and number, you can show the cat only as a kitten and even then the points don't count toward regional or national wins. Even if you decide to neuter or spay your cat, you can show it in the Premiership class if it's registered. Many people who aren't set up to breed cats in their own apartment or home have found that showing a

Premier is exciting and fun. If you do think of going in this direction, you should buy a really nice cat, show quality, because the Premiership class has become increasingly competitive.

MOST BREEDERS ARE NICE

A friend of mine bought a so-called "pet" Seal Point kitten from a southern California breeder. The registration slip was marked in the appropriate box, "Not To Be Bred." For fun, my friend started to show his "pet" as a kitten, and it took off like gangbusters. What happened was that it was a

Left: Gr. Ch. Cannoncats Cyrena of Thaising, a Seal Point female owned by Jill Singer. *Right:* An old-type Siamese. A Siamese coat is short and glossy.

Give your Siamese kitten time to adjust to other pets in your household.

cats and enjoy other people who love cats. New people are always welcome.

PERSONALITY OF KITTENS

Whether you've decided you want a pet or a show cat, personality should be a prime concern. In fact, it might well be your major concern if what you want is a nice companion cat. Most Siamese are extremely affectionate, but occasionally you'll find one who is shy and fearful, maybe even a bit "hissy." Unless you are determined that this is the kitten you want, he probably isn't a good choice. Sometimes such a kitten needs more time before he goes to a new home.

Occasionally a kitten will pick you out. If he comes to you, sits on your lap, purrs, presses, well, it just may be that you're chosen! You'd probably better give in because this is the cat that's going to love you for life. Give the cat a great big ten for taste!

If you're a smoker, especially a heavy smoker, and you are looking at kittens from a non-smoking house or cattery, you may be disappointed to find that the kittens just don't seem to take to you. Cats have a very keen sense of smell, and a foreign or unpleasant odor turns them off. However, many a kitten has grown up healthy and happy

late bloomer. My friend went back to the breeder and asked, "Is there any way we could change the registration slip on this cat?" He wanted to show her to her full potential and to breed her.

The breeder was a nice person. She wrote to CFA and got the registration changed. Well, to make a long story short, the beautiful cat—and she did become beautiful—became a Grand Champion, top of the heap in the cat world.

Moral of the story: do your best to work with someone nice. Some breeders would have demanded lots more money or simply refused to change the registration. Mostly, though, breeders want to help new exhibitors. After all, your cat carries their cattery name and if you do well, it reflects well on them. Besides, if anyone makes a profit on his cattery, I have yet to meet him. Most "cat people" are in it because they love their in the home of a smoker. Your kitten will soon learn to love you despite your bad habit!

HEALTH CONSIDERATIONS

Beware of the kitten who looks as if he has a cold. This could be a temporary situation, as with people, but if you observe runny eyes, whether with white matter or tears, or a runny nose, you'd best not buy the "baby" and take him home. You might want to make arrangements to come back and see him after he feels better if you really like that kitten.

Being small and very short haired, Siamese kittens are more prone to colds than most other breeds. It's not a good idea to stress a sick kitten by changing its environment. Most breeders won't want to sell a kitten that isn't in good health anyway.

Another obvious thing to watch for is a heavy flea infestation. The fleas are liable to make the kitten anemic and weak, to say nothing of uncomfortable, and are also the cause of tapeworms. Most cattery animals are free of fleas, but during the summer, in beach areas, one or two fleas aren't really unforgivable. You will want to get rid of them "pronto," of course, before they start their own breeding program in your house.

Ear mites are another matter. You might suspect their presence if the kitten shakes or scratches at its head or if there is a bad odor or brown wax in the lower (visible) part of the ear. They're treatable, but if the breeder hasn't bothered to cope with them, why get involved with the cat or the breeder?

If the haws, the third eyelid, are up over the eye

This is Rufus, who at fourteen weeks of age has already learned to pose patiently and politely for the camera. Brenda Conner, owner.

(as if the kitten just woke up), you should suspect illness or discomfort of some kind. Haws up, as well as open coats or hair strands instead of nice tight coats (like a fur) are often the symptoms of worms of one kind or another, usually roundworms. Like puppies, kittens are likely to have roundworms, but most

Note the alert expression on the face of this Lilac Point. He is Ch. Leo Zaden, owned by Sibyl Zaden.

breeders will have treated the animals for them if they have symptoms or even if they don't, as a routine preventive measure.

VACCINATIONS?
If your kitten is three to four months old, he should have had at least two vaccinations. Otherwise you'll have to take the kitten to a veterinarian and pay for each of the shots. Many breeders give their own shots, and this should not be a concern to you. It's a great savings for them, and the shots aren't really difficult to administer. Just be certain you know when the kitten had its last shot so you'll know when its yearly booster shot is due, approximately a year later. These vaccinations protect your cat from three of the most feared cat diseases: feline rhinotracheitis, calici, and panleukopenia. Some veterinarians are recommending that cats have rabies shots, also.

ANY GUARANTEES?
Many breeders will guarantee the health of the kittens they sell you. This may be a written or oral agreement. Usually they will insist that you won't decide that the kitten is sick and rush off to any convenient vet. They'd rather that you first consult them and that, secondly, you'd be willing to take your kitten to a vet they know and trust. After all, this is fair.

Sometimes people with a new kitten overreact at the slightest sign of a cold and want to rush the kit off to the vet. Yet they themselves wouldn't dream of going to a doctor for a slight head cold. The breeder can't be blamed for everything that goes wrong over a long period of time. After all, you are providing the food and environment.

Many breeders would replace your kitten if anything fatal happened within a week or two after purchase, even refund your money if you preferred. Some might be willing to pay your vet bill if your kitten was ill with a problem that probably was already present when you bought the baby.

Strange things can happen. A woman who bought a kitten from me phoned to say that it had worms, that her little girl had come running to her with worms in her hand which she'd picked up off the kitchen floor where the cat had been. Her description of the worms sounded like tapeworms, certainly not roundworms, but I just couldn't believe the cat had a tapeworm since she'd never had fleas. I suggested she take some of the worms to the veterinarian along with the kitten and volunteered to pay the bill. She called back, embarrassed but honest, to say that the worms were maggots, which had come from her trash compactor, not from the kitten.

You may notice in looking for a kitten that some breeders advertise their kitten as being FeLV negative. This means that the kittens have been tested and found to be negative or

free from the usually fatal disease, feline viral leukemia. If you're buying an expensive kitten, you may well expect that this test will come free with the kitten. Most breeders don't test all of their pets, however, because the tests are rather expensive. What is often done is that the sire and queen (father and mother) of your kittens are tested once or twice a year, and this is fairly good proof that if they're negative, so will their kittens be negative. Of course, if you really want your kitten tested, you could offer to pay for the test before you take the kitten home.

BEST AGE?

Most breeders prefer to sell Siamese kittens at approximately four months of age. Many would-be buyers have the misconception that if they buy a kitten at six to eight weeks, they can more easily train it to their ways and

A Lilac Point, Gr. Ch. Sanmaur's Lyra, owned by Maurice and Sandra L. Carlson. If you let your pet outdoors, you should always be nearby to supervise him.

Siamese enjoying the outdoors in a sunning and exercise cage.

make it a better pet. Many Siamese aren't even weaned until they are three or four months old.

Furthermore, the first shot or vaccination isn't usually given until the kitten is eight weeks old, the second, a month or so after. The kitten's immune system is then ready for a change of environment, but taking a kitten when it's too young could really stress its health. Siamese are special and will adapt themselves to your household without any real problems whether they're four months or four years old . . . if you give them half a chance.

None of the associations which register kittens allow them to be shown or offered for sale at a show until they are four months old. They are considered kittens until they are eight months old. The prospective buyer might well take a lesson from this.

MALE OR FEMALE?

If you plan to neuter your pet, whether it's a male or female probably doesn't matter very much. Some

breeders suggest that a female usually prefers a male owner, and vice versa, but this is, of course, a generalization. Siamese enjoy co-owners as well as families with children. The more affection, the better, best describes them.

Castrating the male cat is cheaper and simpler than spaying the female cat, but neither operation is very serious these days. Some veterinarians will do the surgery for a nominal fee. The important thing is that you do have your Siamese neutered unless you plan to go into breeding. Otherwise you'll have a spraying male or a howling female. Neither would be good pets.

WHY YOUR SIAMESE SHOULD BE AN INDOOR PET

You'll probably find that no breeder will want to sell you a kitten unless you promise that it won't be allowed to go outside. It might seem that letting a cat out in the sunshine and fresh air would be more natural and beneficial than keeping it in, but it doesn't work out that way.

Your cat could be run over by a car, stolen, or attacked and killed by a wild animal if you live in a rural or semi-rural area. Another danger is the possibility of your cat coming into contact with the leukemia virus, since some outdoor cats have the disease or are carriers. Cats running loose are also likely to get into fights with other cats or dogs and end up with wounds or abscesses. Some insecticides and fertilizers with which a cat may come in contact are extremely poisonous. Unfortunately, there are a few people out there who just don't like cats and enjoy hurting them.

If you buy a kitten who has never been out of doors, you'll be taking a terrible chance to think he can cope with a totally unknown environment. Kittens who have never been outside don't usually even try to get out as long as they have a clean litter box and some sunshine and fresh air. Your indoor Siamese will undoubtedly live a much longer, healthier and happier life than the cat allowed to run outside.

BE SURE TO BRING A CARRIER

If you are seriously going out to buy a kitten, make certain you plan ahead about getting him home. Buy a carrier from a pet store or veterinarian. They come in assorted styles from cardboard to vinyl airlines-approved models. Keep in mind that you'll use the carrier later for taking your cat to the vet, on trips, etc. If you're planning to show a cat, you may as well invest in a substantial, attractive carrier.

A cardboard box may be all right in a pinch, but it can be risky if the kitten gets frightened on the way to the car or in the car. The flaps don't hold very well. Even cardboard carriers are rather flimsy, especially if they aren't carefully folded and put together according to the directions. A breeder told me of a customer who lost his kitten on the way to the car because the bottom fell out of the cardboard carrier. The customer had neglected to put in the extra cardboard piece that makes the bottom more substantial.

A sturdily constructed cat carrier is a necessity for your cat. It should be easily transportable and well ventilated.

You may think that your family member or friend can simply hold the kitten in his lap on the way home in the car. Sometimes it works out. Other times the heretofore gentle kitten panics in the midst of this completely new situation and struggles loose. A kitten under the accelerator or brake is a dangerous matter!

CHAPTER

3

Training and Care

"There are exceptions, but don't be disappointed if your kitten turns out to be a bashful baby for a few days."

ACCUSTOMING YOUR PET TO HIS NEW HOME

You may be tempted to show your new kitten how much you welcome him to his new home by offering food, toys, a new litter box, a scratching post, a bed, and the run of the house. He may respond by hiding under the first bed, refrigerator, chest, etc. he comes across and staying there for hours or days.

After all, the kitten has usually known only one environment, and he may be frightened by all the new sounds, smells, and sights. There are exceptions, but don't be disappointed if your kitten turns out to be a bashful baby for a few days.

It's better if you introduce him to his new home gradually. If you can put him in a quiet guest room or bathroom he may feel less threatened. (Don't forget a litter box.) Feed him there and sit with him there. Encourage him to eat and come to you.

Soon you can let him out into the kitchen or a family room or wherever you want him to spend time. If there are other pets in your home, you may have to referee at first, but most Siamese, especially young ones, interact easily with other cats and dogs. If there is a "hissy match" at first, don't panic. Part of this is establishing what is known as "pecking order" among cats. Sometimes dogs join in too. Your already established pets aren't going to give in without letting the new baby know they are "top cat" or "top dog," but some new kits may try to move in right away, small or not. Most of us waste too much time worrying about the "cat

What a combination! Siamese are almost guaranteed to take to kids and vice-versa. Pictured is Stephanie Berwanger with Ch. Ellian Pandora N. of Bergattos, owned by Liesel Berwanger.

culture." It works out. For the most part, we just need to leave them to their own resources.

A PROPER BED

It's doubtful that any Siamese doesn't feel in his heart that your bed is his bed. If you deny him that, then you must supply a satisfactory replacement. Of course, he'd prefer that this be as close to you as possible, but, chances are, he'll end up on your bed if he's allowed in the same room.

Some cats like to sleep in what is known as a cuddle bed—a soft, comfortable pillow-type bed with raised sides.

If you establish a different place for his own bed, he'll quickly adjust. Siamese love to lie on something—not just the floor or rug—an afghan, a blanket, a towel, an old sweater, the couch, a comfy velvet chair.

When you first bring your baby home, you should beware of drafts. Young kittens can catch colds rather easily, especially under the stress of being in a new home. If it's during the cool season, you might want to give the kitten a cardboard box with bedding. If it's really cool, you can put a heating pad under the box, preferably off to one side in case the box gets hotter than the kitten likes.

Siamese love cuddle beds, the round, fluffy pillows with raised sides, sold at cat shows and pet stores. If you visit a show, you'll see most of the cats lying on these cuddle beds in their cages. If you have more than one cat, they'll enjoy cuddling up together.

Most of this advice is just "spinning wheels" because your Siamese will very likely seek out his own bed, but, beware, it will often be the most expensive piece of furniture in the house. Or, of course, the top of the gas stove!

A LITTER BOX

Very few Siamese present problems about using their litter boxes. Their mothers train them thoroughly, starting at about four weeks, or whenever they are weaned. If your kitten goofs, it may be your fault.

Make certain the litter box is easily accessible. Sometimes kits are off playing and just can't make it in time. Keep the box clean. If the kitten uses another spot, try putting the box there temporarily, gradually nudging it to your desired area. Sometimes other cats or pets make it difficult for a new kitten to use the box.

Your Siamese, like a cat of any other breed, will appreciate a clean litter box. As far as the litter used in the box, your best choice is commercial, deodorized absorbent litter, which can be purchased at your local pet shop. This type of litter is the most effective as far as odor control is concerned. There are also assorted commercial products available that can also help in controlling litter box odors.

A SCRATCHING POST

Fancy or plain, some sort of carpet-covered scratching post is important for the protection of your furniture, drapes, and wallpaper. Your kitten will appreciate and use something on which to flex his muscles and scratch. Mainly, he is flexing his muscles. Usually all you have to do is put your cat on the scratching post if you catch him using the furniture. He'll soon make the change.

If you have the space and money, there are many fancy versions of a scratching post, some extending from floor to ceiling. These have three or four perches or little houses along the way and are a great source of enjoyment to the cats who use them. Your cat may end up using the scratching post as his

Tamago's Icy, a Lilac Point male, demonstrating the comfort of a scratching post that is equipped with a perch. Owner, Greg Elmore.

Your pet shop stocks a variety of litter boxes from which you can choose. Some styles come equipped with a cover, which affords kitty more privacy.

bed. Mother cats have been known to insist on raising their kittens in one of the little houses on the post. They'll just keep carrying them back there. The problem is that if the perch is near the top, the kittens could fall out and be injured before they are good jumpers.

A simple and inexpensive version of a scratching post is a carpet-covered tunnel. Cats love to run through it, stalk each other from each end, lie in it, and get on top and scratch like crazy. It also makes a convenient foot stool for people.

THE BEST TOYS

Siamese kittens and cats love to play, and there are many, many cat toys on the market which may appeal to them. Unfortunately, some

of them are dangerous. Many of the stuffed toys have stick-on or sew-on parts which come off easily and may be ingested. Some toys are filled with styrofoam which your Siamese will soon start eating or depositing all over your carpet. In any event, Siamese are rough on toys. Your best bet is to purchase all toys at your local pet shop.

Catnip mice won't last more than a few minutes. Plastic and fur toys aren't much longer-lived. The plastic cracks and breaks; the fur pulls loose and may contribute to a hair ball in your cat's system.

Cardboard boxes in which you cut openings on the top and sides and then place upside down are a source of enjoyment for many

Siamese cats. A series of boxes is, of course, even nicer than a single box. If you have more than one cat, they'll make their own games. If you have only one, you may enjoy playing cat and mouse by tapping at the various holes.

Siamese cats love to chase balls. There are several types on the market, but the best are those made of safe nylon—Nylaballs®. These and other products are available at your local pet shop.

Since Siamese enjoy jumping and chasing, a dowel or stick strung with a piece of twine or rope can be great fun. You'll be amazed at the quickness of your cat. Sometimes judges at shows offer a peacock feather in order to make a cat show off to its full potential. Siamese who are interested sometimes capture the feather and try to make off with it or break it in half. You may want to try a feather at home, if you plan to show your cat. You don't want to train it to break the feather, but you do want it to show sufficient interest to stretch its neck and body.

There are some things with which your Siamese might want to play but which you must discourage. They include tinsel, foil, cellophane, and moth balls. There are all sorts of rather obvious household poisons,

such as fly strips, most of them fairly well-publicized by now but nonetheless worth mentioning.

POISONOUS PLANTS

Siamese tend to like greenery including lettuce, celery tops, peas, broccoli, and maybe even green beans. Of course, catnip is a supposed favorite, though you may find some like it and some could care less. Actually, catnip turns some cats on to the extent that it is as if they are drugged—not a desirable state. Others find it mildly stimulating.

The important thing is to

Siamese can be inquisitive, and, of course, mischievous! They have an uncanny ability to get into virtually anything in your house.

37

avoid allowing your cats to eat the leaves of poisonous plants. The most dangerous are philodendron; diffenbachia, commonly known as dumb cane; caladium; Christmas Cherry; mistletoe; daffodil and hyacinth foliage; many types of ivy; and often various materials contained in dried arrangements.

Obviously the best answer

A nice alternative would be to grow wheat and oats for your cat. They can be grown in pots, and once the cat becomes used to having them, he won't bother house plants. You'll have to plant a new supply every three weeks or so, but a pound will last a year or more. Of course, the lazy way is to get rid of the dangerous plants and provide some greenery

Training a kitten to obey house rules requires time, patience, and consistency on your part. This Siamese is from Splendid Cattery.

is to try to keep the plants out of the reach of your cats. The common theory is that they eat greenery deliberately in order to make themselves vomit and eliminate hair balls. This may or may not be true. Often they tend to play with a plant just because it's there. Hanging plants are a delightful enticement. Plants in large pots can be fun too. They may, in fact, become a second litter box as well as a source of greenery. In any event, they should not be considered toys.

when you're making a salad or if you have dinner leftovers.

DON'T START BAD HABITS

Well-meaning owners may start a kitten off wrong without being aware of the consequences of their early training. For example, rough-housing with a kitten, encouraging it to scratch and bite, may seem amusing at two to four months, but when the full grown cat decides to please you by repeating the game, you may end up with bloody hands. Never reinforce aggressive behavior with praise or acceptance.

If you don't want your cat to steal food or goodies from the table, don't applaud the cute kitten who snags a potato chip, carries it away, comes back for another, etc.

Another big "no" is giving your cat old socks, sweaters, woolen items, etc., to play with. Not only are some Siamese wool eaters, which can be harmful to their system, but your pet will quickly get the idea that any sock, sweater, or woolen item he finds around is OK to play with. Some Siamese have been known to eat holes in electric blankets and towels. This certainly isn't behavior you'd want to encourage.

BREAKING BAD HABITS

It's probably easier to shut your Siamese off from the kitchen at mealtime than it is to civilize him, but with patience you can get the message across. Otherwise anytime your cat is out, he will jump on your counter or dining table, especially if food is out. Your company may find this offensive even if you don't. Of course, if the cat steals food, there is no question that you have a problem.

Different cats respond to different reprimands. A sharp "no" may be sufficient for some sensitive Siamese;

others respond to a slap with a folded newspaper. A fly swatter is a strong deterrent to many cats. If you can plan ahead, a squirt from a water pistol may get the message across. It's best if the cat is left to believe the water comes from God or nature or, well, anyway, not just you.

After a while, the cat should respond even to the sight of a folded paper or fly swatter. Never, never use your hand to administer punishment. It's confusing and could be hurtful. Cats associate your hands with petting, feeding, grooming, and administering to their health. A paper or fly swatter is neutral; your hands are not. Cats won't tolerate physical punishment in the sense that dogs will. The important consideration is that the cat understands what is allowed and what is not allowed. Always keep in mind that Siamese are

For this six-week-old kitten, security is a stuffed toy animal. (If you provide your cat with toys such as this, make sure that all sewn-on parts are securely attached.)

anxious to please. Hurting anything but their feelings will do more harm than good.

Consistency must be at the heart of any training. If your couch is to be forbidden, don't ever let your cat sit on it. Otherwise the cat becomes confused. Don't allow your Siamese to sleep in your bed with you sometimes but not other times. He's bound to cry and scratch at the door. If you don't want him begging at the table, never, never, never, feed the cat morsels of your food. If you want to give him a few table scraps, put them in his bowl on the floor or wherever you usually feed him.

Your Siamese will do his best to please you, but he has to understand what pleases you.

YOUR TIME TOGETHER

Siamese are very much creatures of habit. Make certain the routine you set up with your cat or kitten is one you enjoy and can continue to enjoy.

Don't feel guilty about leaving your kitten alone if you work or are away during the day. A companion cat or dog would be nice, but cats sleep a surprising number of hours, day and night.

A friend once rejoiced that she had a vacation and could spend time with her kitten. She was disappointed to find the kitten slept right through most of the anticipated togetherness time.

What your cat will come to count on is the special uninterrupted time you give him in the morning and evening when you feed him and, hopefully, show your affection and interest in him. It's, as they say of children, not just the quantity of time but the quality.

If you come home from work and like to sit down and have a drink and some goodies, your Siamese will be right there. Both you and the goodies will be attractive to him.

I sold a kitten who loved peanuts. The new owner went me one better and fed him cashews, which, of course, he liked even better. Siamese are also noted for their love of cheese and assorted chips. They are really party cats.

Whenever you're giving time to your Siamese, you should first look sharply and feel him all over to make certain all is well health-wise. To the cat, it will seem to be just another form of petting, but it could save you all kinds of problems if you notice any early symptoms. For example, it takes only seconds to notice flea bites, the onset of ringworm or a skin problem, runny eyes, dirty ears, small injuries, a broken tooth, or, with a kitten, uncomfortable teething, or acne on the chin, especially of a lilac or blue. This is not to suggest that Siamese are more prone to health problems than any other breed, except for being prone to colds when they are kittens. The same quick examination would be advisable for any cat or dog. Sometimes we tend to take their health for granted.

Siamese enjoy conversations with you, and never, never can you be accused of talking to yourself. Many will answer with a "meow" to their names. Few owners can resist talking to their cats, and Siamese, especially, relish a good dialogue. Certain key words seem to be understood, such as "snack," "dinner," "good kitty," "bad kitty," "no."

Some Siamese will run to the phone when it rings, and if you sit down to talk, they may jump on your lap. They act as if they're in on the conversation. Unfortunately, they have been known to knock the phone off the hook if they're home alone.

It's flattering, though occasionally irritating, to find that your cat follows you like a dog. They just hate to see you go away, once they've had you to themselves. It's wise to make certain you don't leave them behind in a closet or guest room from which they

have no access.

By all means, if you have a sunny spot in your house, make it accessible to your Siamese. He'll love to lie and bask in the sun. The spot is even more prime if it includes a view of the out-of-doors. Even if you have to add a perch, scratching post, or window seat, you should do it. Of course, your Siamese may find his own spot on top of a TV, book case, or piece of furniture that provides a space in the sun.

Second to a sunny spot

The eyes of a Siamese—vivid blue in color—are one of the most remarkable features of the breed. Pictured is Gr. Ch. Angkor Rose Chip Ahoy, owned by Betty White, a CFA judge.

Some fanciers prefer to keep a pair of Siamese so that the cats can be companions to each other. This duo is Ch. Camelot Zaden and Ch. Candida ("Didi") Zaden. Sibyl Zaden, Zaden Cattery, owner.

which is also warm is a warm place. Favorites may include the top of the TV (rated safe by those who know), the top of the dryer when it's on, the top of the refrigerator, and, of course, available space in front of the heating system. Many Siamese like to perch up high because it's warmer up there.

A COMPANION CAT

A friend for your Siamese, especially another Siamese, is certainly a big plus. They'll play together by the hour, thus insuring that they get the exercise sometimes missing for the bored, lonely cat.

Any cat, whatever breed, or a dog can provide friendship. It's best if at least one of the pets is young when they're brought

together. It may take a few days for them to become friends, but soon they'll be eating and sleeping together as well as initiating a few pranks together.

A companion animal is not a requirement, but in a household where no one is around most of the day, another pet can bring a lift to the life of your Siamese. Some owners fear that their animal will be less affectionate if they bring in another pet, but this isn't really true. Human companionship is an absolute must for a Siamese and most other pets too. Another pet can't take the place of a human.

TRICKS EASILY TAUGHT

Most animal behavorial experts rate the Siamese as a very intelligent breed of cat. Certainly it is the most extroverted and anxious to please. These are the characteristics that make it unusually trainable.

Retrieving Most Siamese love to retrieve. Wadded up paper balls are as good as anything. They'll soon learn not only to return whatever you throw but to drop it at

please you.

Jumping Up On You Most Siamese will jump up on you if you say their names and put out your arms. At first they may not make it all the way up to your chest or shoulder, but usually they tend to learn to land in your arms, with a little adjustment on your part.

Siamese kittens are delightfully resourceful when it comes to amusing themselves.

your feet, in your hand, or in your lap. At first you may need to sit on the floor with your kitten and throw the ball only a short distance. Praise him lavishly if he picks it up and heads in your direction. Soon he'll get the message. Be sure to praise him verbally and pet him each time he brings you the ball. At times he may find his own piece of paper and pester you to death with it, but, after all, he is trying to

The only problem with this trick is that some cats enjoy it so much that they do it without a signal. If you've just stepped out of the shower or have on a new blouse or shirt, you may not appreciate the invasion. Some cats like the trick so much that they're likely to jump on anyone who comes into the house, ready or not. For these reasons, this may be a trick better left unencouraged.

Bowing Or Praying Lowering the head between the front paws is a nice trick, most easily taught to a Siamese that tends to make the gesture on its own. A cat with a runny nose or eye may repeat the gesture over a period of days. Be sure you praise your cat whenever it makes the gesture, such as "Oh, good, Delilah. You're so smart!" And pet her and encourage her to do it again so that she knows what's going on. "Pray, Delilah. Pray again!" And more praise. Soon she'll do it on command for dinner, praise, etc.

Sitting Up Sitting up or standing on their hind legs is so natural and easy to Siamese that neither can really be thought of as learned tricks. They are born knowing how. All you need to do is to teach them to do it on command.

They'll stand up for food, then drop to a sitting position as you lower the food. They'll do the same for a string, feather, or toy, which you hold aloft. Many do it on their own in order to reach something above their height, such as a hanging plant. They'll also sit up in order to see out over a barrier such as the lower covered portion of a screen door. Their balance is almost uncanny.

Leash Training The main purpose of a leash is to be able to take your Siamese outside for a walk. Some people also use them to let a Siamese out on the patio or back yard and yet keep them restrained. The trouble with this is that they are a ready prey for any other animal that might come along. Also, they tend to get accustomed to being outside and may then become an unhappy indoor cat who rushes to the door every time it's opened.

A walk on the leash is different in the sense that your Siamese is with you the whole time. If there is trouble, you can pick him up and carry him away. Actually, cats, even Siamese, are not as good on a leash as a dog. They are easily frightened and somewhat skittish even after weeks of experience. It's probably best to walk with the cat close to home or in your own yard, if you are determined to take him out. A strange dog, traffic, skateboards, etc. may scare the cat to the point that even if you pick him up, he is too terrified to know what he is doing. One owner I know had to throw his own sweet cat in the garage until it calmed down and could be handled.

It should be made clear that a cat requires a harness with its leash, not a collar. He could easily slip out of a collar or, if it were pulled tight, choke himself. It's

At six weeks of age, a Siamese kit's curiosity in the world around him is quite apparent. These kittens are from Tohpao Cattery in Southern California.

best to accustom him to a harness before you attach a leash. He'll probably turn somersaults and brush against everything in the house to get rid of the "darned" thing, but he will come to ignore it. That's when you might try adding the leash.

The only time I've ever found a leash useful was on a cross-country trip when we wanted to stop for lunches in various parks and bring the cat out for some fresh air and a luncheon snack. The cat enjoyed the small freedom involved after being in a carrier in the car all day.

USING THE TOILET

There are various products on the market designed to teach your cat to use the toilet . . . your toilet, that is. Not the litter box. The only problem is that they just can't seem to learn to flush the toilet. Siamese are stars when it comes to this sort of toilet training, but whether it's worth the hassle is another question. It does require a special potty top, at least to get them started, which would have to be removed whenever a human used the toilet. An occasional cat will start using the toilet on its own with no encouragement, but this is unusual. A few will also use your wash basin, which isn't the nicest surprise when you have guests.

CHAPTER 4

Grooming

YOUR CAT DEPENDS ON YOU

Although Siamese are one of the easiest breeds to maintain in terms of coat, you must keep in mind that there are other concerns involved in grooming. You are all your cat has—that is, you and your household. That's why it's important that you also trim his claws, keep him free of fleas, parasites, and skin disorders, clean his ears, and, occasionally, his teeth. Of course, if you're rich, you could have the vet or a groomer do all this for your cat, but it's really not that difficult to handle things yourself. Your Siamese will prefer that you work with him.

You'll soon come to enjoy helping your Siamese, a proud pet, to keep himself up in the same sense that you keep yourself up. He'll do his best to keep his own coat clean, but if he is to be an attractive and satisfactory house pet, he needs some assistance from you. If you praise him lavishly during and after grooming, he'll soon learn to strut around and show off as if he recalls his royal background.

BRUSHING THE COAT

Your Siamese will purr all through the time you brush him, once he becomes accustomed to it. Because his coat is short, he really doesn't require much brushing, except for the possibility that he may get hair balls in his stomach from licking his own loose hair. Brushing out the dead hair will prevent shedding on your furniture and clothes, a special problem during the seasonal change from summer to winter.

An interesting question

(joke) is how the Siamese manages to leave his dark hair on your light clothes and his lighter hair on your dark clothes!

The best brush is a two-sided rubber one, sometimes known as a show brush. The contoured side works best with the Siamese. You need to be careful with this brush because not only will it remove dead hairs but live coat as well. You can create dips or hairless spots if you brush too hard or over and over in the same spot.

An exhibitor at a show was brushing her Siamese while she talked to a friend, and, suddenly, cried out, "Oh, no, I've made a hole on his tail!" Sure enough, she'd been so engrossed in conversation that she'd gone over the same spot until she'd pulled out all the hair.

Any natural bristle brush can also be used, but be careful of synthetic brushes which may be too harsh for your cat's tender skin.

It's a good idea to set your cat on a newspaper, preferably on a table, so that you can easily brush all parts of his body without fussing or straining. If the coat seems dry or full of static, you may want to use one of the many coat conditioners for sale at pet stores. Their main purpose, of course, is to enhance the coat for showing. They

should add sheen, reduce static electricity, and make the coat lie closer to the body.

PREVENTING HAIR BALLS

Closely related to brushing is the prevention of hair balls caused by the cat's licking his own coat or the coat of another cat. The usual symptom is coughing or coughing and vomiting,

The time and care that you devote to your pet will be reflected in his overall appearance. Owner, Susan Ross.

An ordinary bristle brush will help to keep the dead (soon-to-be-shed) hair out of your cat's coat, but most breeders use a rubber brush, obtainable at pet shops.

usually with hair in it. The cat might also pass hair in its stool. Siamese are less likely to get hair balls than most breeds, but they certainly aren't immune to them. Brushing out excess hair is the first key to prevention.

Fortunately there are readily available products which help a cat to cough up its hair balls. They are very palatable and usually work within 24 hours. Petroleum jelly can also be used. Mixing chicken fat or bacon fat in the cat's food every week or so also helps prevent hair balls and will add sheen to the coat.

TRIMMING CLAWS

Pet stores sell special clippers for cats' claws. Unless you're showing your Siamese, the main reason for clipping its claws is the protection of your furniture and clothes. If the claws are so long that they catch on the rug or click on the linoleum, they are probably uncomfortable for your cat.

Clipping is easy. All you need to do is to retract each claw, making sure you have good light, and snip just below the visible vein. Sometimes the clippers seem to pinch and shatter the claw in layers, which may hurt the cat a bit, but, with praise, a Siamese will tolerate this clipping quite well. Making certain your clippers are sharp also helps.

THE DECLAWING CONTROVERSY

Owners and veterinarians alike disagree about the advantages and disadvantages—to cat and owner—of having a cat declawed. There is no question that it protects your furniture and drapes, but whether it's fair in view of the physical and emotional complications your cat may suffer is questionable. Most cats can be trained to a scratching post. If not, your only alternative may be to have the claws of the front paws removed, that is, if you are determined to keep the cat.

The operation, which is done under anesthesia, involves cutting across the first joint of the paw. The feet are bandaged for two or three days to help prevent hemorrhaging. Walking will be painful for a week or longer. Sometimes one or more claws regrow but are misshapen. There are other possible physical complications.

The declawed cat may also develop emotional problems. He may become distrustful of his owner and vet. Since he is almost defenseless, he is apt to be nervous. If he feels threatened in any way, he may bite.

Vets and owners in favor of declawing minimize the possible harmful effects of the surgery (onychectomy),

claiming that only rarely are there unfortunate side effects. In fact, they say their cats are less nervous when declawed because they are no longer subject to being punished or yelled at for destroying furniture or drapes.

It should be noted that a cat who has been declawed can be shown in only a few of the registering associations and not in CFA.

BATHING

If your Siamese is strictly a home pet, you may never have occasion to bathe him, but people who show their Siamese often bathe them in order to add silkiness and luster to their coats.

Occasionally a cat may get into something that leaves him sticky and foul-smelling, and, in this case, a bath may be helpful. A bad flea infestation or skin disorder may also require a bath. Area washing may be indicated in cases of facial acne or stud tail.

Check your pet's paw pads for signs of irritation and abrasions.

In terms of grooming, the Siamese requires minimal maintenance.

Since bathing removes most of the natural oil from the coat—even with feline shampoo—it's important to bathe a cat four or five days before the occasion on which you want it to look especially nice. This allows time for the oils to return naturally. A dry, fluffy coat, for example, is not going to win any beauty contests in the show ring.

The best bath is well-planned and moves quickly along. If you have a double sink, you should use it, kitchen, bathroom, or laundry room. Fill one side with approximately six inches of warm water. Have shampoo, a plastic cup, and two bath towels conveniently at hand.

Make certain you choose a mild shampoo, preferably one especially for cats. If, of course, you're bathing because of fleas or skin problems, you'll be using a special shampoo. Pet stores offer a variety of products.

It's to your advantage to patronize a pet store rather than a grocery market, where there is often a very limited selection of brands and products.

Have your cat's claws clipped short since he may panic at first and try to climb out of the sink via your arms and shoulders or anything around the sink he can sink his claws into.

Talk to your Siamese in a reassuring way as you start his bath and praise him as he stands (possibly shuddering and howling) in the sink water. Wet his whole body down by pouring warm water from the plastic cup over his back and tail, but not his head. Gently lather him with shampoo, being careful not to get soap in his eyes and ears. Sometimes a scared cat may react favorably by being pressed down into the warm water of the sink.

The main thing is to hold the cat firmly, allowing no

foolishness, to keep talking, and to keep moving right along. Once you've scrubbed the cat down, turn on the faucet on the other side of the sink, making certain the water isn't too cold or too hot and then simply stretch the cat out lengthwise and hold him under the running water, rotating, as if he were on a spit. Make sure you remove

Siamese find them frightening. You may want to comb or brush the cat's coat after he's almost dry. Not only is this a reward for tolerating the bath, but it will make the coat look even more finished when it's dry.

COPING WITH FLEAS

With all the successful new products available, there's no reason to tolerate a flea

Siamese are fastidious when it comes to keeping clean. Here a mother cat meticulously grooms her youngsters.

all the soap. Turn off the water and press excess water from his paws and tail.

Now comes the part your Siamese will enjoy. Wrap a towel around him and carry him to a warm or sunny area. Dry as thoroughly as possible. Probably you'll need a second towel to finish up. Try to keep the cat in a warm area until he's totally dry. Some breeds will tolerate a hair dryer to speed things up, but most

infestation in your house or on your cat. There are sprays and bombs which kill not only the fleas but the eggs as well. It's important to understand that fleas jump on a cat or dog to ingest a quick meal of blood but spend most of their time on the rug, couch, or bedding of your animal. That's why removing fleas from the cat at any given time doesn't solve the problem.

It is imperative that you get rid of fleas as quickly as possible, since a bad infestation can cause anemia and even sudden death in young kittens, and tapeworms in cats of any age.

Some Siamese have a flea bite allergy and suffer much more severe itching and problems than normal. As a result, they scratch and bite their skin until they create raw, red areas which can become infected. A flea bath may be necessary to help a cat with a flea allergy.

You must be extremely careful about using any kind of flea dip or shampoo on kittens under four months old, however. A friend used a dip purchased at her grocery store on some 14-week-old kittens, four Seal Points and one Blue Point. They were all severely burned, and the Blue, the prize of the litter, suffered such pain and trauma that she had to be put to sleep. In the resulting law suit, the breeder was paid damages, but, of course, it didn't bring her kitten back. "I should have suspected something," the breeder said, "when I noticed the dip was removing all my nail polish." The product did not and does not carry any warning on its label although the breeder is busy writing to the Environmental Protection Agency, her assemblyman, congressman, etc.

Many exhibitors use a flea comb to remove fleas from the cat's coat. This fine-toothed comb literally catches the fleas in its teeth so that they can be dropped into a bowl or cup of soapy water or alcohol.

Flea sprays and powders can be helpful, but most Siamese don't like them. They especially dislike the sound of the spray can. A sprinkling of powder on the cat's bed will probably be tolerated best.

Flea collars can be dangerous to the sensitive skin of a Siamese. If you want to use one, it's best to take it out of its wrappings and leave it in the open air for approximately ten days. Even after that, when you put it on your cat's neck, check daily to make certain there is no hair loss, redness, or irritation under the collar. Never use a flea collar in conjunction with other flea control methods. The build-up may be toxic.

KEEPING EARS CLEAN

Cleaning your cat's ears weekly or bi-monthly with a cotton swab dipped in mineral oil or baby oil will usually insure against ear mites as well as clean out any dark wax in the lower ear. All you need to do is work the swab gently into the crevices of the visible part and press lightly down toward the ear drum.

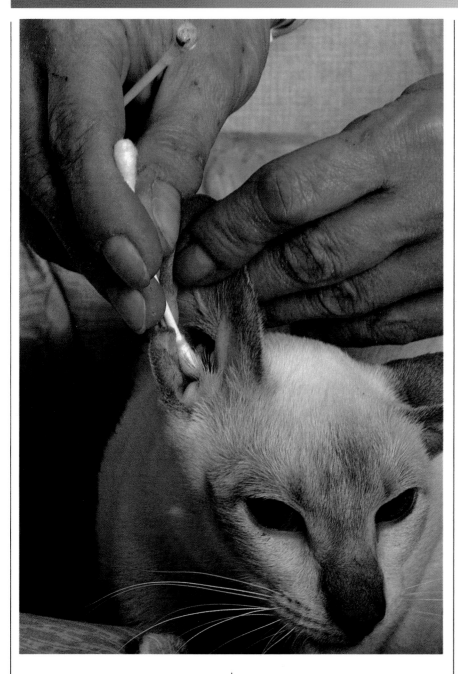

A cotton swab can be used to clean your cat's ears. Clean only the visible part of the ears and never probe into the ear canal.

Symptoms of ear mites include your cat shaking his head or pawing at his ears. You may also notice dark material that looks like coffee grounds in the ear. Mites are transmitted by another cat who is infected. Kittens may get them from their mother. Once you suspect your cat has ear mites, you are going to have to treat him beyond mere grooming. You should put the oil in his ears daily. If you don't seem to be curing the problem, you should take the cat to the vet, who will prescribe a regimen of eardrops.

CHECKING THE EYES

Unless your Siamese has a cold, his eyes should be clear and bright. Occasionally you'll notice a bit of "sleep" in his eyes, which you can easily wipe

Be sure to exercise caution when it comes to selecting household plants, as some can be poisonous to cats.

out with a piece of tissue. If he has some white matter now and then, you'll need to remove it with a swab. Some Siamese eyes are rather deeply set and trying to use a tissue just doesn't work out. Of course, if the eyes should continue to be a problem, you should consult your vet.

ACNE

Although your Siamese may not be a teen-ager, he may be subject to acne on his chin or lower lip. This occurs most often on the lighter Siamese, Lilacs and Blues. At least, it is more visible on them. It is a bacterial infection, probably caused by a build-up of food particles on their sensitive

skin. If not attended to, the area may become inflamed and exude pus.

The best treatment is prevention. If your cat has this tendency, wipe his chin and face clean with a cotton ball and warm, soapy water or rubbing alcohol at least once a day. If the condition has progressed to a large area or seems sore, be kind. Don't rub hard. It will be painful to the cat. If you can remove the blackheads by pressing, go ahead and do so. Applying warm compresses first can make it easier and less painful.

In extreme cases, the vet may have to shave the area and remove the blackheads and, if there is infection, prescribe an antibiotic. Generally speaking, though, it's not a difficult condition to handle if you keep on top of it.

STUD TAIL

As the name suggests, this is a condition which affects the tail of an unneutered male cat. Similar in appearance to facial acne, stud tail is caused by a secretion from the sebaceous glands on the upper part of the tail, near the body.

In its early stages, it looks like a dirty, waxy patch under the fur. If untreated, stud tail will progress into blackheads and festering pustules, which may cause the color of the tail to lighten, and, eventually, the fur to fall out. Secondary infection may set in. As with acne, early treatment is the answer. The tail should be scrubbed daily with a medicated soap or a mechanics' soap and dried thoroughly. Getting rid of the waxy buildup is the significant element.

Of course, you could have the cat neutered and eliminate the whole problem!

KEEPING TEETH CLEAN

You can brush your cat's teeth if the two of you have the patience and perseverance. Just as with people, an excessive build-up of tartar on the teeth can cause receding gums and infections of the gums and teeth. Dry cat food (crunchies) will help prevent the build-up of tartar.

Probably the simplest way to brush the teeth is to dip a piece of gauze or cloth in a salt and baking soda solution (one teaspoon of salt and one teaspoon of baking soda in a cup of water) and scrub the cat's teeth back and front. Veterinarians sell beef-flavored toothpaste, which can also be used. It all sounds very nice, but most Siamese owners don't seem to have much luck with this brushing routine.

The alternative is to watch for signs of tartar and sore teeth, such as bad breath, teeth turning brown,

dropping food while eating, quivering jaws, or inflamed gums. If you observe any of these things, you'd probably be better off to let your vet deal with them. Often all that's needed is a thorough cleaning of the teeth, something you just can't do yourself without anesthesia and know-how.

Some say the longer the head of the Siamese, the more likely he is to have dental problems, but this has yet to be proven. The most significant factor in any breed of cat or dog is misalignment. Some cats are born with missing tooth buds and will never have a full set of teeth, but usually this doesn't affect their health.

Cozy nooks and crannies are especially appealing to kittens. These Siamese look right at home in their carpet-covered hideaway.

Nutrition

"Leftovers from your meals are a welcome addition to the cat's dinner. They add nutrition too."

You can undoubtedly find as many recommendations for the diet of your Siamese as you can find interested owners. Each will swear by certain foods, vitamins and minerals, and, of course, the manufacturers of commercial foods would all have us believe theirs is the very best.

One thing seems certain; Siamese, more than any other breed, seem to need multi-purpose vitamins, in addition to good nutrition, for optimal health.

WHAT TO FEED

Most Siamese do fine on commercial canned food and kibble (dry food). However, there is increasing concern about the animal by-products, preservatives, and dyes in some of these products. It's important to vary the flavors of both the canned and dry so that your cat doesn't get hung up on one variety to the exclusion of all others. The kibble helps keep their teeth free from a plaque build-up and is also a convenient food to leave out in case feeding time is to be delayed.

Cottage cheese or almost any cheese is a great favorite with most Siamese. According to Jeanne Singer, a top American breeder (Singa Siamese), they particularly enjoy an imported, aged cheddar cheese! Be careful about milk. It often has a laxative effect. If your Siamese begs for milk, you may find he can digest canned milk, mixed half and half with water.

Leftovers from your meals are a welcome addition to the cat's dinner. They add nutrition too. You may be surprised to discover that your cat enjoys not only

This old-type Siamese may have a short muzzle compared to current winners, but the profile is certainly flat. Pictured is Dbl. Ch. Kim-Kee's Loki of T'Lu, a Lilac Point owned by Janet R. Beardsley.

scraps of meat but peas, green beans, lettuce, cantaloupe, avocado, spaghetti, rice, and assorted Oriental foods, especially if they're covered with soy sauce. A steady diet of leftovers is not advisable though, because it will lack the balance prepared cat food offers. Feeding dog food more than very occasionally is also inadvisable because it lacks some of the nutrients needed by cats.

Egg yolks are another special treat, raw or cooked, and help to keep the coat shiny. Since cats can't digest egg white, it's best not to give them that part of the egg, though it won't actually do any harm if it has been cooked.

HOW MUCH TO FEED

You should keep your Siamese lean and lithe, as he is meant to be. If you happen to have an "old style" cat, you may find that he'll just naturally insist on more food and tend to carry more weight.

In general, adult Siamese shouldn't be fed more than one-quarter to one-half of a six-ounce can of food per meal. Kibble should be limited to approximately a handful per cat. If you're supplementing with other goodies such as leftovers, cut down accordingly. Many Siamese tend to be chow hounds, with the result that they gain more weight than they should for health and beauty's sake.

You'll probably want to set a routine: kibble in the morning and canned food at night or vice versa. You can limit your Siamese to one meal a day and feed more, but most tend to like a morning and evening feeding.

If your cat acts hungry but seems to be too heavy, try putting him on a diet. For example, feed less kibble and give him cottage cheese or some other lower calorie substitute, just as you might for yourself.

VITAMINS AND MINERALS

The diet of your Siamese should be supplemented with a good veterinarian-recommended multi-vitamin and mineral product. These will vary. Not all vets agree on which product is best. The easiest form to administer is the powder because it can be mixed in the moist food. Some Siamese find vitamin tablets so palatable that they'll eat them like candy.

Human multi-vitamins, purchased at a health food store, are also fine, though you must be careful about the dosage. Choose one that is low-potency and get the best advice possible on the quantity to feed.

WATER

Make certain your

"You should keep your Siamese lean and lithe, as he is meant to be."

Siamese always has plenty of fresh water in a clean bowl. The water should be changed every day, and the bowl should be scrubbed out. Recently some veterinarians, particularly those involved with reproductive problems in cats, have advised that bottled spring water be given rather than tap water. The nitrites in many water systems are harmful to the cat. A rule of thumb might be that if you can't stand to drink your own city water, then you shouldn't offer it to your cat.

BECOMING A DIET EXPERT

If you are really concerned about the diet of your Siamese or if the cat should develop special health problems, you might want to do some research on your own. Some commercial foods contain animal by-products you'd rather not know about, as well as harmful chemical additives, such as dyes and preservatives.

BHA and BHT, used in many foods to preserve the fatty contents, have been investigated by various food and drug agencies and have already been banned in some countries. Fortunately, not all companies add these preservatives.

Red dye no. 40 or sodium nitrite is added by many companies to appeal to the eye of the owner. Unfortunately, as attractive as the red meat or multi-colored crunchies may look, the colorants fed over a period of time are suspected of causing cancer and birth defects. Red dye no. 40 has been banned in Canada and most European countries. An added irritation is that if your cat happens to vomit on your carpet after eating a product containing this dye, you may find the stain almost unremovable.

The highly-touted semi-moist foods for cats contain propylene glycol (about 10%) to keep them moist. Many vets report that the semi-moist food, which most cats love, eventually causes diarrhea, itchy skin, and dull coats.

Just as people are becoming increasingly concerned about the chemicals in their own food, so should they be concerned about the food their pets eat. At the least, if you read a label with an over-long list of chemical additives, avoid that food.

Many pet stores carry health food for cats, which does not contain preservatives or dyes. Sometimes, representatives of health food companies have a booth at cat shows and offer literature and free samples. This is an excellent chance to find out if your cats like its taste, because what good is any food if they won't eat it? Although some of the health foods cost more per pound, usually your Siamese requires a smaller amount, since all of the food can be utilized by the cat's system. Some commercial foods show a high protein percentage on the label, but, alas, some of the protein cannot be utilized and is simply wasted.

THE WRONG STUFF

Feeding any food exclusively is a danger because not only does it limit the nutrients taken in but it may result in a cat becoming finicky when any

"Feeding raw fish only is bad because it contains an enzyme which destroys vitamin B1."

other food is presented.

Certain foods are especially dangerous. Feeding liver only can cause lameness. Feeding tuna only can cause a vitamin E deficiency called steatitis, which could prove fatal. Feeding raw fish only is bad because it contains an enzyme which destroys vitamin B1. It could result in weight and appetite loss, heart disorders, and even convulsions and paralysis. If you cook the fish, all is well, providing you remove the bones.

Though cats in the wild kill and eat birds, including the bones, feathers, and innards, the brittle cooked bones of fish and fowl fed to your house cat can splinter and cause damage to its throat or intestines.

VITAMIN C

In addition to a regular regimen of vitamins and minerals, you may want to try vitamin C with your cat, particularly if it has any health problems. Originally, it was believed that cats, unlike humans, could manufacture all of the vitamin C they needed, but in the last decade research veterinarians have proved conclusively that cats can't produce all the vitamin C they need, especially in times of stress.

The role of vitamin C in cats' diets has been researched by many

Bahn Yindee Patrick, a Blue Point male, bred by Judith Deutschman and owned by Stephanie Grant.

veterinarians, including Dr. Wendell Belfield, director of the Bel-Mar Orthomolecular Veterinary Hospital (San Jose, California), a clinic which specializes in disease prevention and treatment of small animals through nutrition.

Research by Dr. Belfield and others indicates that vitamin C improves immunity and is highly effective in treating viral diseases, including the most feared of all, feline leukemia. Vitamin C has been shown to turn leukemia-positive cats negative. Of course, the doses used to counteract already existing viral problems are "mega."

Because of the abundance of literature on the subject, more and more breeders are including vitamin C, usually in the powdered form of ascorbic acid, as a daily supplement for their cats and kittens. The multivitamins available on the market won't include a significant amount of vitamin C. If you decide to try vitamin C, you'll need to buy it separately. The easiest form to administer is the powdered ascorbic acid.

The recommended dosage for normal maintenance by Dr. Belfield is 500 to 750 mg. per day. If the cat gets diarrhea, you know that you should cut back. Most products will tell you on the label what the dosage translates to in terms of a part of a teaspoon.

As with humans and the research of Dr. Linus Pauling, there are dissenters who question the validity of the vitamin C research.

CHAPTER

6

Health

Noticing early on that your Siamese doesn't seem to feel up to par can save you lots of worry and grief, to say nothing of vet bills. Some obvious signs of possible illness are lack of appetite, diarrhea, a tacky coat, the haws (third eyelid) up, general listlessness, sneezing and/or runny eyes and nose, coughing, scratching, and hair loss.

Other behavior to be *very* concerned about is a cat's sitting in the litter box and straining for long periods of time and a cat that hangs its head over the water bowl but doesn't drink. If home remedies and tender loving care don't seem to improve the cat's condition in a day or two, it's time to get your Siamese to a veterinarian.

CONSISTENT VETERINARY CARE

If you're lucky enough to find a veterinarian who really knows and cares about cats, you should use the services of this person for all your cat's health needs. This person will then have all the records on your cat: his vaccination dates (if given there), the date for his yearly booster shots, care given (such as wormings and examinations), all of which could be helpful if your cat ever had a serious illness.

TAKING A CAT'S TEMPERATURE

If your Siamese appears to be ill, one of the most significant things you can do in many cases is to take his temperature. Probably if you call the vet in terms of emergency treatment, the first thing his office will ask is if you know the cat's temperature.

A thermometer should

A Siamese kitten is the embodiment of impishness and curiosity.

Geneticists also refer to it as a "restriction factor."

If a Siamese gets a wound or cut or fungus infection, the then-exposed area is colder than the surrounding area, and the new hair will grow in darker. After the next molt (sometimes almost a year), the new fur will match its own area.

Sometimes when a queen is bred, the male will grab her neck so hard that he'll puncture her neck and pull out fur. I had male brothers who practiced on each other so much that I had to give up on the little guy I was showing because of hair loss.

Waiting and waiting for the proper-colored fur to return can be tiresome. There's no question that the younger, lighter-coated Siamese tend to do best in the show ring. Meanwhile, you're waiting, and your Siamese is getting older.

A possible solution is the application of the gel from an aloe vera plant directly onto the affected area three days in succession. This is also reputed to help what exhibitors call "ticking out"—the loss of point color on the head after a Siamese has had a fever or been on antibiotics for a few days.

Since the aloe vera gel straight from the plant is bitter, be careful when applying it around the cat's eyes or nostrils.

By the way, this plant (genus *Agave*) is a readily available succulent that has long been recognized for its ability to minimize burn scars. It's easy to keep an aloe vera in a pot on your patio or a somewhat sheltered area of the yard. It can also be planted in the ground. Commercially packaged aloe vera gels can be purchased in health food stores and drug stores.

never be inserted into a cat's mouth for fear that it may be broken. An ordinary rectal thermometer is best. Lubricate the end of the thermometer with mineral oil or petroleum jelly and insert gently into the cat's anus. Hold it there for two to three minutes. Try to keep the cat quiet while you do so. The normal temperature is up to 101.5 degrees (39°C); anything above this suggests trouble.

A temperature under 100 degrees (38°C) is also a serious sign (except in a queen about to deliver). The cat should be wrapped in blankets or put on an electric heating pad until it can be taken to the vet. You may need to administer one teaspoon of water with one-quarter teaspoon of brandy.

COLDS

Siamese are fairly subject to colds, especially when they are young, because of their short coats. Actually all cats are subject to colds in the same way that humans are, although it's doubtful that the two are transmissible. Avoiding drafts and shifts in temperature are probably the best ways to avoid these colds. Don't do your Siamese a favor by leaving the air conditioning on while you're away. They don't need it or like it.

Don't panic because your

A proper diet, exercise, and regular veterinary care are important factors in maintaining your cat's good health. This Lilac Point is from JoRene Cattery, owned by Irene Brounstein.

cat gets a cold. Do you rush to the doctor every time you get a cold? Although aspirin in general is a big "no" for cats, a baby aspirin or a quarter of an adult aspirin can be administered *once* to reduce the fever.

Some vitamin C and a dab of mentholated petroleum jelly on the cat's nostrils will help clear up the congestion. You may need to clean his eyes and nose with a damp tissue (with warm water) to remove secretions.

Make sure you keep the nostrils as uncongested as possible because a Siamese without a sense of smell is a Siamese without an appetite. This is a good time to quicken the appetite with strong-smelling treats such as jack mackerel or tuna.

If the cold doesn't clear in a few days and your cat has a fever, you definitely should consult your veterinarian. You may be faced with a virus that is beyond home remedies.

HOW TO ADMINISTER MEDICATION

If you are administering a pill or capsule, it's easier to get it down your cat's throat if you moisten it with butter, margarine, or some oil appealing to the cat. If you're lucky, it will just slip right down. Beware though; many is the time I've pilled a cat and praised it for its cooperation, only to find the pill on the couch or carpet a few minutes later. They can be sneaks! Some cats even hold the pill in their mouth for several minutes and then, "spit-too-ee," let it loose.

You can buy gadgets that flip the pill into the back of the cat's mouth, but probably the easiest method

A lovely litter of Tohpao Cattery kittens from Gr. Ch. Angkor Rose Cathay Au Lait of Tohpao.

because they do love to be praised.

DOES MY CAT HAVE WORMS?

Symptoms which might suggest that your Siamese has worms vary with the type of worm involved, but one certain method of finding out if the cat has worms (and what type) is to take a feces sample to your veterinarian.

Some knowledgeable breeders routinely worm their young kittens, but for the average owner to go to a pet store, buy worm medicine, and administer it without any clear idea of what may be wrong with the cat could be dangerous. Some of the common worm medicines are as hard on the cat as on the worms you are hoping to get rid of.

is just to get the cat in your lap or on a table with his feet down firmly, tilt his head, and let loose, as far back as possible on the center of the tongue. Then hold the cat's mouth shut while keeping the chin pointed upward. It may help to massage the throat to encourage swallowing. A sudden blast of air sometimes might cause the cat to swallow.

Liquid medicine in an eye dropper or syringe is probably the easiest to administer. Basically all you have to do is pull down the lip on one side and insert the eye dropper or syringe. Once you've squirted it in, your cat doesn't have much choice if you hold its mouth shut.

By the way, whatever medication you give, be sure you praise your cat thoroughly for allowing you to administer it. Some Siamese will actually seek you out to be given more and more medication

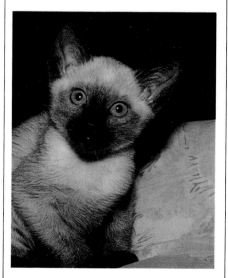

Roundworms These are among the most common worms, particularly in

kittens. Feline youngsters can get roundworms from their mother's milk, from sharing a litter box with other infected cats, from eating rodents or birds, or even from contact with large black water bugs, which may deposit eggs in the cat's water bowl.

Often your cat will show no real symptoms of roundworms, the larvae of which migrate through the liver, lungs, and trachea before lodging in the intestines. When the infestation is heavy, however, you may notice the haws up over the eye, pot belly, coughing, diarrhea, tacky coat, and lack of muscle tone. If it looks as if your cat vomited up thin, circular masses of spaghetti, you can be sure he has roundworms.

Since the life cycle of roundworms is two to three weeks, you need to worm or have the cat wormed at intervals in order to clear up the condition.

Tapeworms Tapeworms are also an intestinal parasite,

common in cats. If your Siamese is an indoor cat, he'll most likely get the flea tapeworm if he gets a tapeworm at all. This is caused by his swallowing fleas, which carry the larvae. Although your cat may be non-symptomatic, you may notice he has a tapeworm by finding flat, whitish worm segments in the feces. Some may still be alive if fresh. You may also notice dried segments (rice-like) around the cat's anus, in the feces, or anywhere the cat has been.

There are actually four types of tapeworm, but the same treatments work for all of them. The old treatments for tapeworms were messy and uncomfortable for the cat, but a new injection given by the vet makes quick work of the problem. Trying to handle the worming yourself may prove frustrating, since you accomplish nothing if the head of the tapeworm is not released from the intestine.

Ringworm This problem has nothing to do with worms at all. It's a skin condition caused by a fungus infection which involves the hair and scalp or skin of the cat. It's important to recognize that ringworm is one of the few feline problems which can be passed from animal to human, human to animal, animal to animal, and human to human. Cats may be carriers and not show any of the classic circular inflamed areas (accompanied by hair loss). Usually ringworm appears first on the head, neck and front legs but can be anywhere and if left untreated, will spread all over the body. Most ringworm can be diagnosed by the vet when he views the fungus under an ultraviolet light. He can also make a culture of the fungus, but this could take from three to fourteen days to be definitive.

New medication has brightened the prognosis for ringworm, though it is still a maddening development in a cattery or home where more than one cat resides or where there are children, since they are much more likely to end up with the fungus than older people or older cats. The problem is that the infection itself, which can be transmitted by one hair, has a life span from thirteen months to five years. Some say longer. Oral tablets of griseofulvin can be obtained at the drug store and used for both humans and cats. They should not be used on pregnant cats, however. The other most potent medication is PVP-iodine diluted about ten to one and applied directly to the affected area as many times a day as possible. (In severe cases, you may have to give

Calkin's Syzygy of Tohpao, a Seal Point male. Owner, Brenda Conner.

your cat a bath in this medication.) A topical antifungal agent for animals is also helpful in controlling the spread of the spores. Cats infected with ringworm or any fungal infection are forbidden to be shown at a cat show, but, unfortunately, some owners fail to heed this rule. It's easy to notice ringworm on a Siamese because of its short coat, but on a long-haired Persian it's another matter.

BITES AND ABSCESSES

Cats may occasionally be

A mother cat will frequently employ this method of discipline with a wayward kit.

bitten or stung by an insect, especially if they are allowed out of doors. Bees, wasps, fire ants, and spiders could be cause for a trip to the vet. Pain, swelling, and redness are the usual symptoms. The bite of a black widow spider or scorpion could make your cat very sick indeed.

The most frequent bites are those from another cat or occasionally a dog. The most dangerous bites are the deep puncture wounds that are the result of the long canine teeth. The big scare with an outdoor cat would be that the wound may have been inflicted by a rabid animal. Increasingly, rabies shots for cats are recommended by veterinarians.

Any bite—deep or not—if it causes a break in the skin, may result in an abscess. That's why it's important to pay attention to any wound. First aid should include dripping hydrogen peroxide

onto the open area; then an antiseptic such as merbromin or an antibiotic ointment should be applied.

An abscess occurs when a bruise or puncture wound closes up and doesn't drain. It may go unnoticed for several days, but suddenly there is swelling and fever. If the bacteria spreads into the bone or blood system, treatment may become complicated. At best, you'll need to have the veterinarian lance the abscess and flush it out with antibacterial solution. Usually he'll send home some of the solution so you can continue the treatment, as well as antibiotics to be given orally.

DIARRHEA

Simple diarrhea is no cause for alarm and may be caused by overeating, a change in diet, or an emotional disturbance. The best at-home treatment is probably a chalky binding agent, one teaspoonful per five pounds every four hours or so. Opinions vary on the exact dosage.

In general, it is best to cut down on food or withhold it entirely for 12 to 24 hours; then to switch to very bland foods such as cooked chicken, baby food, rice, or cooked eggs. If you suspect a change in diet may be responsible, you may want to change back. If you want to make a switch-over, do it gradually, mixing in a bit of the new food with the regular food until the cat's system seems to have adjusted.

Diarrhea that continues longer than three days without improvement or bloody diarrhea should not be allowed to go on and on without a trip to the veterinarian. If you can take a stool sample to the vet

help alleviate the situation.

Cats can be given an enema if the severity of the constipation warrants it, but this is a task best left to your veterinarian.

WOOL EATING

Actually, Siamese who eat wool enjoy other fabrics also, much to their owner's discomfiture. My own have devoured electric blankets,

Lilac Point female awaiting the arrival of her kittens. Owner, Phil Morini.

when you bring in the cat, this could help him make a diagnosis more quickly.

CONSTIPATION

Hair balls can cause constipation, as can improper diet, over-feeding, and lack of exercise. The easiest way to deal with this condition is to feed the cat milk or cream and/or to add some form of oil to his food. Liver also helps to loosen the bowels. A quality dry food, which has more bulk than canned foods, can also

towels, socks, cellophane, the stuffing from toys and pillow beds, and almost anything available. It's only fair to admit that Siamese are of a breed most likely to be a so-called "wool eater."

Friends who had such a Siamese locked him in the bathroom away from everything tempting the night before he was to be shown, hoping to protect him and to keep his weight down. What did he do? He ate the entire lining of the waste basket. It's a miracle

that more of these cats don't end up with intestinal disorders. Usually they don't. Often they outgrow the condition.

Boredom, loneliness, and nutritional deficiencies such as a lack of lanolin or certain minerals have all been blamed. Sometimes the problem is solved by feeding the Siamese a larger quantity of food or a better-balanced diet with vitamin and mineral supplements. Large chew toys sometimes help.

DENTAL PROBLEMS

It's important to do all you can to keep your cat's teeth clean and free from plaque. If your Siamese rejects crunchies or other hard foods and begins to eat only soft foods, you may suspect that you have a cat with a tooth or gum problem. He could react in the same way if his tonsils were sore and inflamed.

Often you can look into the cat's mouth and find that he has a broken tooth or sore gums. A few of the tiny front teeth missing, upper or lower, isn't really significant.

Sometimes, a cat will never get its full set of teeth. This usually isn't a health problem but could affect the cat's chances in the show ring.

TEETHING

Kittens begin to get their deciduous teeth at two to three weeks and have a complete set of them by four to five weeks. It's the period from three-and-a-half to five months that a kitten may have fever, swollen glands, loss of appetite, and sometimes diarrhea, due to cutting his permanent incisors and canines.

Most kittens have little or no problems. You may find the baby teeth in or around their scratching post or on the carpet before you know what's happening. Then again, one kitten from a litter of others without problems may grind its teeth, clutch at its mouth with a paw, and act almost crazed. This is most often because the second teeth have come in, but the baby teeth haven't fallen out.

Sometimes you can pull an obviously loose tooth, but if it doesn't seem loose or the cat won't let you help, you may have to wait it out a few days or go to the vet. A continuing situation could force his teeth out of alignment.

FELINE UROLOGICAL SYNDROME (FUS)

FUS is a general term including cystitis, bladder inflammation and/or infection, and a more severe condition, generally called kidney stones in humans.

The most common symptoms for either include straining in the litter box with little or no results, bloody urine, urinating in unusual places, licking of the genitals, an ammonia-like smell to the urine, apparent pain when being picked up, and a general listlessness as the condition continues.

Contrary to popular opinion, female cats as well as males can be affected, though the young male cat is the most likely candidate. If what the cat is suffering from is no more than infection, your veterinarian can prescribe antibiotics to clear up the problem. However, if the cat is obstructed with stones you are faced with an emergency condition, because the cat will be unable to urinate and the resulting toxins could kill him within 48 hours.

FELINE INFECTIOUS PERITONITIS (FIP)

Most of the latest research on FIP indicates that the "I" (infectious) should be

removed. It is certainly not as highly contagious as originally believed. Breeders used to insist not only on a leukemia test but also on an FIP test for a queen that was to be brought to their male. Very few bother with the FIP test anymore because no matter what the test shows in terms of "titers," as the degree of exposure is expressed, it doesn't seem to be meaningful.

FIP is indeed a serious and usually fatal viral disease, but the point is that it is not as infectious as originally believed nor as diagnosable by test as originally believed.

The disease takes two forms, the wet and the dry. In the wet form, you will observe first what appears to be a cold with sneezing and runny eyes and nose.

Lovely profile study of Gr. Ch. Tosa Mahogany, a Chocolate Point female.

Most cats will throw off these symptoms and become immune to the disease, although they will show titers on being blood-tested. Others who don't pass it off become fatally ill, often with difficulty in breathing and a bloated abdomen filled with fluid. They soon fail to eat and lose more and more weight. Trying to save them is a heartbreaking cause—you may keep them alive for several weeks by force feeding and tender loving care, but in the end, they just can't make it.

The dry form of the disease takes so many different forms that it's almost impossible to diagnose. The real problem is that it often affects specific body organs, with the result that tests may show a problem with that organ but the diagnosis may not be complete. The symptoms vary as greatly as the possibility of different organs being affected. Some might include convulsions, lack of coordination, diarrhea, vomiting, drinking too much water, not eating, and general listlessness.

The only advice worth following is to take your cat to the best veterinarian possible and hope for some other diagnosis. In a situation where it's clear that your cat has FIP, some vets may recommend euthanasia.

FELINE LEUKEMIA (FeLV)

This virus has become the big scare among breeders and exhibitors. It causes more deaths than any other cat disease and is almost always fatal. If you decide you want to breed your Siamese, you'll undoubtedly be asked to have your queen tested for leukemia. In fact, you might well wonder about the breeder who doesn't insist.

A vaccine is available for this disease. Check with your veterinarian regarding the advisability of having your cat innoculated. The shot in itself is not curative. Also, the vaccine should never be administered to a pregnant female. It could cause deformity or death to the kittens. Usually, kittens who have tested negative are innoculated at two months, three months, six months, and, after that, with a yearly booster. Some breeders prefer to test their cats regularly—and there are several excellent tests—rather than to vaccinate because they are concerned about possible side effects. Some breeders who don't want to risk infection of their cattery may place leukemia-positive cats in one-cat homes, where they may thrive with no apparent symptoms for several years.

Some symptoms of FeLV include frequent colds, respiratory problems, abscesses, tumors, and

reproductive problems. Basically, FeLV-positive cats have a weak immune system. Unfortunately, a cat may be a carrier and not exhibit any of these symptoms. There is, as yet, no clear evidence on how the virus is transmitted.

FELINE IMMUNODEFICIENCY VIRUS (FIV)

A new concern for cat lovers is a virus, not unlike FeLV, which has probably been in existence for some time but has only recently been isolated and renamed. Originally it was called Feline T-Lymphotrophic Lentivirus (FTLV), as this virus was found to be in the same family of lentivirus to which the human AIDS virus (HTLV) belongs. For this reason, the media gave the public the mistaken impression that cats could transmit AIDS to humans.

Each animal species has its own lentivirus which can not be transmitted to other species. A human can't give a cat AIDS any more than a cat, sheep, or cow can give a human AIDS.

There is a blood test for FIV that identifies the presence of antibodies to the virus. However, as yet there is no vaccine or sure cure, although cats who are showing symptoms may be helped to lead fairly comfortable lives for five years or so with good veterinary care.

Symptoms may include gum infections, sneezing, diarrhea, ear infections, weight loss, reproductive problems, and lethargy associated with anemia. FIV seems to be more prevalent in older cats, indoor/outdoor cats, cats in a multi-cat household, and the male of the species (three to one).

An old-type Blue Point Siamese. Note the remarkably stocky build of this cat.

CHAPTER

7

Preventing and Handling Injuries

"Given the opportunity, some cats will lie dangerously close to a fire in a fireplace or sit on a very hot floor furnace. They do enjoy heat."

Most first aid for cats wouldn't be necessary if their owners took consistent, intelligent precautions, though cat-proofing one's home isn't the easiest thing. Siamese cats are among the most active and curious of all breeds, which means an even more strenuous regimen is required to avoid accidents.

Burns

Electric stoves are a very real problem because turning off a burner doesn't immediately stop the transmission of heat. Many a hungry cat has scorched its paw pads (goodbye to a show career) by jumping up on a still-hot burner. If you can't find or fabricate a cover for your stove, you should leave a pot over the burner until it has cooled off. The best idea might be to try to make the stove a great big NO.

This isn't easy. My own Siamese would rather sleep on the gas stove at night than any place else. One of them used to insist on pressing so close to a pilot light that he often singed the fur on his front paws. Given the opportunity, some cats will lie dangerously close to a fire in a fireplace or sit on a very hot floor furnace. They do enjoy heat.

Other concerns should be electrical cords and outlets. If a cat bites through a plugged-in cord, he'll suffer severe and disabling mouth injuries. Electrical outlets should be plugged off with plastic covers when not in use. Otherwise your cat could press his nose to the outlet or possibly spray into it and cause a fire. If you have a spraying cat, you may find that your outlets

"An ounce of prevention is worth a pound of cure" is an adage to be kept in mind when it comes to your pet's safety. Siamese are inquisitive and will investigate *anything* that catches their attention.

will short out and have to be replaced.

Another potential burn hazard is an iron with its tantalizing cord. If a cat is left alone with a hot or still warm iron, he could pull it off the ironing board onto himself or start a fire in the rug.

One of the saddest things I've heard of was the death of a gorgeous show Siamese who somehow managed to get the lid off of a deep fryer filled with hot oil and fell into it. The deep fryer was cooling off and had been pushed way back on the counter to avoid an accident, but the accident happened.

In any case of a burn injury to your cat, do your best to apply cold water by dipping the foot or injured area, applying a cold compress, or an ice bag. If the cat seems to have only first degree burns with mainly just redness, the wound will heal itself with no real problems.

A second-degree burn is more serious and will involve blistering as well as redness, and a third-degree burn involves charring with blackened or whitish skin. Both second- and third-degree burns should be treated by a veterinarian because your cat has lost fluids, and he also may be in danger of infection. He may need to be contained in order to prevent further injury if his feet are involved.

POISONS

Beside poisonous plants, there are many, many innocent-appearing items in your kitchen, bathroom, and laundry room cupboards which could be dangerous to your cats. Areas containing cleaning materials such as bleach, drain and oven cleaners (with lye), deodorant sprays, dry cleaning products, dyes, floor waxes, and the like should be cat-proofed, as should medicine cabinets containing aspirin, talcum powder, boric acid, tranquilizers, etc.

Pesticides are among the most insidious poisons for cats, especially those pesticides containing antu (used in rat and mouse poison), arsenic (used in snail and insect poisons), strychnine, thallium, and warfarin (used in rat poisons), nicotine (used in plant and poultry sprays), and the chlorinated hydrocarbons used in some products.

Almost all insecticides and weed killers are dangerous. Hopefully your Siamese is an indoor cat, and these dangerous poisons are stored outside in a garage or tool shed.

COAL TAR PRODUCTS

These too are common around the garage and

A Blue Point queen pictured a few days before delivering her litter.

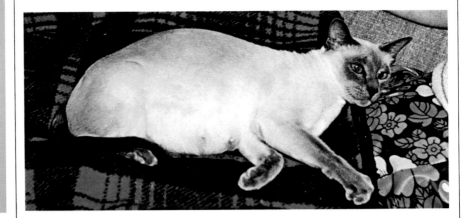

Gr. Ch. Cannoncats Abelard, a Seal Point male owned by Austin Turner of Moqui Cats in Phoenix, Arizona.

house and can be very harmful. Included in this category would be fuel and motor oils, gasoline, turpentine, creosote, dry-cleaning products, and petroleum distillates. Some household bleaches and cleansers contain coal tar. Floor waxes are toxic until dry.

ANTIFREEZE

The trouble with antifreeze is that cats love it. If thrown or dropped on their fur, they'll lick it off with great enjoyment, but it is deadly poison.

Unfortunately, this poison has been used at cat shows by sick people to kill off competition or slow down the cat fancy in general or who knows? The only antidote is an alcoholic beverage, such as brandy or vodka, administered to the cat with a syringe or medicine dropper as quickly as possible. Any antifreeze left on the cat's coat should be rinsed off with soap and water and the cat wrapped in a towel and rushed to the vet.

SYMPTOMS OF POISONING

These may include vomiting, diarrhea, salivating, trembling or convulsions, hard breathing, appearance of pain, and sometimes a paralysis of the hind quarters. If your Siamese is having convulsions, be extremely careful. It's best to handle him with a towel or blanket since he may harm your hands by biting or scratching without really knowing what he is doing.

Although symptoms are variable based on the specific poison, there usually isn't time to sit around and analyze the situation, anyway. Grab the cat, the container of whatever you think it has ingested, and, if vomitus is present, a good sample on a paper towel or whatever is

"Many an unsuspecting cat breeder has endangered his cat by administering aspirin over a period of time, even baby doses."

handy, and head for the veterinarian.

If you're not sure what poison your Siamese has ingested, it's difficult to suggest what first aid to attempt. In situations where there will be a delay in getting veterinary help, an emetic to induce vomiting could save the cat's life. Often the container of a dangerous product tells you the best emetic or antidote. A call to the nearest poison control center might give you the information you need.

POSSIBLE EMETICS

One of the simplest emetics, if it's available at the time of emergency, is a teaspoonful of hydrogen peroxide solution (3%) right from the bottle with eye dropper or syringe. This can be repeated two or more times until vomiting occurs.

Plain table salt is another helpful emetic. You can dissolve it in one cup of warm water per teaspoon (difficult to get down the cat's throat) or try putting ¼ teaspoon plain salt on the back of the cat's tongue.

DON'T USE AN EMETIC IF . . .

Your cat has been poisoned by a toxic agent which has already burned his mouth and possibly tongue. He will be salivating profusely, may have convulsions, obvious mouth

and tongue burns, and perhaps shock.

Among the toxic or corrosive agents in this category are carbolic or muriatic acid, alkalis such as lye or other drain cleaners, and petroleum products.

Incidentally, never, never use paint thinner or turpentine to remove paint from a cat's fur. The cat can get sick from the toxicity even through unbroken skin. If you must use a little of a petroleum product, be ready to bathe the cat immediately afterwards.

THEY MAY SEEM INNOCENT BUT . . .

Some other products to watch out for are baby powder or talcum powder, which, if ingested by licking or inhaled through the lungs, can damage internal organs, cause pneumonia or lung congestion.

Boric acid powder, sometimes used in the treatment of ear mites and by breeders of white Persians to counteract discoloration from tearing, can be highly toxic to cats if taken internally. If they walk in it and then lick their feet, they could suffer fatal bleeding of the stomach and intestinal tract.

Many an unsuspecting cat breeder has endangered his cat by administering aspirin over a period of time, even baby doses. Some vets say that a half of a regular

A beguiling pair of Siamese kits. Even though your favorite feline gives the impression of independence, he needs looking after.

aspirin over one or two days for pain is all right, but continuing the dosage is very dangerous to a cat's internal organs.

It won't be much of a holiday if your Siamese decides to investigate the Christmas tree and ends up eating some tinsel or other decoration likely to ball up and obstruct his intestines. Glass ornaments, so very breakable, are also dangerous if swallowed. Some of the styrofoam-filled decorations are all too easy to eat. Unfortunately, the whole idea of a Christmas tree with decorations and lights may be a problem with one or more Siamese cats. I've known them to jump up and knock the whole tree down. Then, again, older Siamese may just stand back and admire, awaiting their gifts from under the tree.

Moth balls or moth crystals can be deadly poison to cats who are attracted to them and gobble them up. Unfortunately, some well-meaning people suggest that a practical way to prevent cats from using a spot other than their litter box is to place a package of moth balls there. This could be a terrible problem. Spraying vinegar is most likely to solve the problem without harming the cat.

CHOKING

It's not true that Siamese and most other domestic cats can chew, swallow, and digest the bones of fowl and fish without possible choking, even if the bones are cooked. This isn't to say that the cats may not growl in glee over these bones, but they simply aren't safe for them to eat.

A cat could choke on an over-large dry crunchy, particularly if he's an eager eater, though often his own salivation will moisten the piece enough to make it swallowable before you're faced with an emergency situation.

Other enticing and dangerous household objects best not swallowed include parts of cat or child toys, such as sewn-on eyes, coins, matches, buttons, beads, small pieces of wood—oh, you name it! Among the scariest is a piece of thread, which may or may not have a needle attached.

If you believe there's a chance that your Siamese could have swallowed a needle *and* thread, you should try to find the needle in its palate or throat, but if you can't get cooperation from the cat or you can't find the needle, you'll need to get to the vet for X-rays in most instances. If the thread comes right out of his mouth and you're certain you haven't allowed any access to a sewing basket, you may be safe, but you'd better watch the cat closely for signs of distress. The needle could be almost anywhere in the cat's system.

GENERAL SYMPTOMS OF CHOKING

These are rather obvious. The cat may paw at its mouth, cough, drool, or gag. Similar symptoms may be shown by a Siamese with a hair ball, a cold (they do get sore throats), or a habit of purring so loud and long that he starts coughing or has a sort of dry heaves. Kittens four to five months of age who are cutting teeth may also scare you with their grinding and pawing, but, again, there is no emergency.

HOME TREATMENT

The best immediate measure for choking is to grab the cat and hold it upside-down, rather roughly. If nothing happens, shake him a bit. If still nothing is ejected from his mouth and he continues choking, press on his chest with both hands (while he's still upside-down). If these measures fail, you may want to try to inspect his mouth in case there's something obvious stuck in his teeth or across his throat, but if the cat acts half-crazed, it's

"The best immediate measure for choking is to grab the cat and hold it upside-down, rather roughly."

probably foolish to risk your fingers. Some books recommend trying to remove an obstruction with needle-nosed pliers, but I question what may result. Remember, the cat is already panicked, and chances are, so are you. It's better to let the vet deal with the problem!

One of the smartest things I ever did was to put a child-proof safety latch on the door of the cupboard in which I keep my kitchen trash. Prior to that, no matter how carefully I closed the door, my neuter managed to work it open, thus making the trash available to him and all the other house cats (usually during the night, of course!).

The moral of the story on poisoning and choking is obvious: make certain that storage places containing harmful agents aren't available to your Siamese.

ARTIFICIAL RESPIRATION

The chances of your ever needing to use artificial respiration on an adult cat are fairly slim, but if you do any breeding, you may find it useful on a newborn kitten who just doesn't seem to take hold and start or continue breathing. An adult cat who has suffered severe electrical shock might also need artificial respiration.

All you have to do to give a cat artificial respiration is to place your own mouth

over his muzzle (nose and mouth) and exhale gently. When the cat responds and breathes, remove your mouth so that he can exhale. Keep offering a short puff of air and a short wait. It should work out to about 12 breaths per minute. With a newborn kitten, make certain the lungs are clear of mucous before you resort to artificial respiration. It may not be necessary at all.

HEAT PROSTRATION

Never, never leave your Siamese closed in a car during warm weather. You may think that leaving the windows open a little will make it all right, but the rise in temperature inside a car can be as much as 40 degrees in a matter of minutes. If the cat is enclosed in a carrier, the

Gr. Pr. La Vond's Kheen Dhani. This Seal Point neuter is owned by La Vond Thompson.

81

Seal Point Gr. Ch. Terlin Starquest owned by Terry and Linda Little.

heat will be even more intense.

A cat unknowingly locked in a closet, attic, or patio area could also suffer heat prostration. Symptoms are panting, foaming at the mouth, vomiting, dilated pupils, an inability to stand up, and, finally, total collapse.

The best first aid is fresh, cool air and damp towels pressed against the cat's body. An ice pack to the head might help too. If the cat is unconscious, you'll need the help of a veterinarian even if you are able to bring it back to consciousness. The cat may be very dehydrated.

EVEN THOUGH THEY MAY LAND ON THEIR FEET . . .

When they fall, cats have an astounding ability to right themselves in mid-air so that they land on their four feet. This doesn't necessarily mean they won't have an injury, however. What's funny about Siamese is that despite their long, graceful bodies, they can sometimes take a clumsy fall from a counter or TV and land with a thud on their stomach or back. Fortunately, it doesn't usually hurt anything but their vanity. Siamese don't like to be laughed at or made fun of.

One of the record heights for the survival of a falling cat onto a hard surface is 18 stories. Such falls occur most often from balconies or windows with loose screens. A Siamese queen in season can wreak havoc on a screen that isn't well-secured. I've even heard of a queen scratching her way up the chimney and through the fireplace onto the roof.

Cats that fall a distance may end up with head and chest injuries, broken teeth, or broken legs. There could also be internal bleeding and shock. A fall from any real distance normally requires professional help.

IN CASE OF HAIR LOSS

The points of the Siamese are accounted for by the fact that the actual one-colored coat is sensitive to cold. The points being the extremities, that is, the coldest parts of the body, become darker. This is known as the Himalayan factor.

CHAPTER

8

To Breed or Not to Breed?

"Many stud owners aren't willing to offer breeding service to an unregistered queen."

Some of the reasons people think of for breeding a queen are based on myths. No, your female will not be healthier and happier if she has one litter before being spayed. No, watching kittens being born is not necessarily an educational (in the best sense) and enriching experience for your young children. What if she has a painful breech and gets panicky? What if one or more of the kittens is abnormal, mewing and crying until they die or you have to put them to sleep? What if all the friends and relatives who absolutely "loved" your female weren't as serious as you thought about wanting one of her kittens?

IS YOUR SIAMESE REGISTERED?

If your cat isn't registered with at least one association, breeding is probably not a good idea. Even if you breed her to a male who is registered, the kittens are still unregisterable.

Many stud owners aren't willing to offer breeding service to an unregistered queen. Selling the kittens may be more difficult than if they had the possibility of being registered. They will all have to be sold as pets, even if they are of show quality. There is a futility involved in the situation. If you really want to breed Siamese, you should purchase a registered cat before you get involved.

IS SHE WORTH BREEDING?

Although this may sound like a mean question to someone who has a cat of which he or she is wildly fond, nonetheless it is a question which needs to be

A Siamese is svelte and lithesome in appearance. Pictured is Gr. Ch. Two Sisters Bryn Mawr, a Blue Point female owned by Lynn Y. Sakai and the author.

asked. Many pet-type kittens and cats have wonderful personalities, but their "type" (appearance) leaves much to be desired. If you attend a few cat shows and look at the Siamese, you'll quickly discover whether your cat is up to standard or strictly a pet.

Probably the next step is that you'll decide that you don't care, that you like your cat's type better than those ugly, old, pointy-nosed, skinny things being shown. This is a fairly common reaction, but, in a way, it becomes a defense mechanism. My cat's better than your cat! No matter what . . . because I love my Siamese.

You should consider the Siamese standard in trying to determine whether to breed your cat. If she has crossed eyes and a kink tail, you'd surely decide against creating more of these unshowables. You should consider her color, body structure, and head type in the same manner.

Most serious breeders are concerned with creating the most perfect kittens possible. Not all will be show quality, but, hopefully, some 20% may be, and the others will be nice, too—just not quite as perfect. If, after looking at other Siamese, you are still uncertain about whether your cat is worth breeding, you might want to ask a breeder or judge to help you evaluate her.

PLANS FOR THE KITTENS

Don't assume that just because you have a litter of kittens, buyers will beat a path to your door. It's best to plan beforehand how you will sell or place your kittens.

Of course, if your queen is registered and you breed to a nice stud, you may find many buyers interested in the show-quality kittens, that is, if they know you have them. The problem is that most of us want to keep the best and sell the pet-quality kittens.

Usually you'll have to advertise or sell your kittens at a cat show, both of which cost money. Keeping in mind that you probably shouldn't sell before four months (the youngest they can be sold or shown at a cat show), the best age in terms of the kittens' health, you're going to be investing some money in cat food, vaccinations, and occasional health problems.

This is not meant to be negative, but it is important that you recognize that, as adorable and fun as the kittens may be, there is more than pure pleasure involved. They can be rough on your furniture and drapes until they are trained to a scratching post.

On the positive side, I've bred females whose owners fell so in love with the kittens that they refused to part with even one of them. They kept the whole litter! A litter of four or five Siamese welcoming you home as they run toward you with tails up is unquestionably one of the most endearing sights you'll ever see! They are something!

THE QUEEN IN SEASON

The calling of a Siamese queen who wants to be bred has driven many an owner to the veterinarian for a spay appointment or to a breeder for a proper sire. Siamese are one of the most vocal and vehement breeds when it comes to being in season. By the way, it isn't a good idea to spay the queen when she is in season. Her organs are swollen because the blood vessels are in a state of dilation. This makes the surgery more difficult.

Part of the behavior will also include treading with their back legs as if they are being bred, stiffening their backs when being handled, and generally acting out the breeding they desire. They'll also press and purr around anyone who'll put up with it. Some also urinate here, there, and everywhere during this time.

Even if your female is an indoor cat, the males in the neighborhood may leave a momento on your front or back door—some of their spray. It's amazing how

"Siamese are one of the most vocal and vehement breeds when it comes to being in season."

scent and sound travel with these cats! This is especially true in summer if you have open windows or doors.

Your female should not be bred earlier than ten months of age. The kittens will steal the calcium and minerals she still needs for her own continued growth.

If your queen starts coming in season as early as five or six months, you have a problem. A bath may help, but only for a short time. Often she'll cycle in and out every couple of weeks, summer or winter. This strain, especially if accompanied by lack of appetite, could be worse than letting her go ahead and breed. In this case, it's extremely important that you supplement her diet with calcium and all the good stuff.

THE QUIET QUEEN

Once in awhile a queen appears to be less highly sexed; that is, she doesn't make it obvious to her owners when she is in season. This would not be unusual behavior for a Persian, but it is for a Siamese. Needless to say, this makes it difficult to breed her. If, of course, you own your own stud and can simply let them be together, your problem will likely be solved. The male knows exactly what's going on and will know when he can breed to her. Trying to ship her or

take her to someone else's stud could be a real problem. If you're not certain she's in high heat, it's hardly fair to expect the male and its owners to handle her. She'll be miserable, too, stuck in a foreign environment and in a cage, which she probably isn't used to.

THE LATE BLOOMER

There are queens who don't have their first season until they're a year-and-a-half or older. This is no cause for panic. Some lines just seem to require more maturity. Others may start their seasons early but may

The elegance and personality of the Siamese cat have made it one of the most popular of all feline breeds.

be unable to conceive until two or so years later. Often very young mothers who do conceive have only one or two kittens. This could be disappointing if you've paid a high stud fee.

STUD CATS

Keeping a male cat whole (unaltered) involves a lot of work and patience. Most Siamese males spray and must be kept in cages. Even those who don't spray are a problem if you have female cats around who aren't spayed. They'll breed them with or without your permission.

Because of the spraying, the males are usually kept in a separate cattery, away from the house. Ideally, they'll have outdoor runs for nice weather, since being caged all the time isn't exactly fun for them. Some males, especially young ones, mew and call for females, just as females call for them. Some breeders use their stud cats until they're four or five years old, then neuter them and place them or give them more freedom to run in the house or cattery. Unfortunately, some never stop spraying. It has become a habit. In this instance, they really need an outdoor run.

Because the males do require extra work, most people aren't interested in keeping them or simply don't have the proper

"Keeping a male cat whole (unaltered) involves a lot of work and patience."

facilities. That's why it may be wiser to find a suitable stud, pay the fee, and have your female bred if you've decided you really want her bred.

If you have a male cat whom you intend to keep as a pet, it's best to neuter him before he starts the spraying habit, usually by nine or ten months. Some males mature earlier than others.

FINDING A SIRE

Many breeders who offer stud service don't advertise the fact because they are very selective about the queens they want used with their male. You may see ads which say "Limited stud service" or "Stud service to selected queens." This is exactly what they mean.

There are several reasons for this. First of all, health is an important consideration. A stud owner doesn't want to deal with the owner of a queen who would be careless about the health of the cat. His male could become ill. He may have several other cats in the same cattery who could also be infected. Naturally, a leukemia-positive test will be required, but this is just one aspect of health. If you are a well-known breeder with a good reputation, the stud owner can be certain you won't bring or send a queen with a cold or virus or vaginal infection.

If he cares about his stud

cat, he doesn't want to expose him to a female who is unusually aggressive or so neurotic that she might attack and hurt the male. Some queens are just so plain spoiled that they won't tolerate being caged with a male, even if in high heat. No breeder wants to be stuck with a situation like this. Remember he has to feed the cats and clean the cage and litter box. He'd rather not have his fingers bitten in the process.

Another concern is that owners of stud cats want their males to produce the best kittens possible. If your queen isn't likely to produce nice kittens, or at least not with this male, you may get a turndown.

You may find the best possibility for a good sire at the cattery from which you bought your kitten. Even if this breeder doesn't offer stud service, he may be able to recommend someone who does and who would have a suitable male for your female.

HOW DO YOU DECIDE WHICH MALE?

It doesn't require a course

A successful breeding program requires time, money, and dedication. A conscientious breeder strives to create the best possible specimens of his selected breed.

in genetics to figure out that the best male for your female would be one who appears to have strengths to correct her weaknesses. For example, if her ears sit too high on her head to complete a perfect triangle, find a male with nice, low-set ears. If her eyes are a bit light in color, pick a male with deep blue eyes. If her body is rather thick-set, choose a male with fine bones and long legs.

All of this sounds as if it should work, but there are other factors to consider. This involves studying the pedigrees of the two potential breeder cats. What you should look for are ancestors in common. That's why it's often best to go back to the breeder from whom you purchased your kitten. You're more likely to find cats there with ancestors in common.

This is called linebreeding or inbreeding, depending on how close the relatives may be. Breeding brothers to sisters, fathers to daughters, or mothers to sons isn't generally recommended, but the breeding of more remote relatives has certain advantages over outcrossing to a cat with whom your female has no common ancestors. The results of outcrossing are completely unpredictable. Two beautiful cats may produce a ho-hum litter because of recessive

genes which the breeding brings out.

Linebreeding almost invariably results in kittens as good or better than the cats being bred. Of course, this is a worthless idea if the line from which your kitten came wasn't much good to begin with. If, however, it's a well-known line with its share of grand champions, breeding back into it will certainly be your best chance for a nice litter. Study your cat's pedigree well; you may be surprised to find more studs around with similar lines than you thought. Talk to breeders at shows; join a Siamese breed club if possible. Once other exhibitors see that you are serious, you'll find new opportunities opening.

WHAT COLORS DO I WANT?

Naturally, you want to choose a male who will produce with your female the color of kittens you most want. This can get complicated unless you have a breeding chart, but in general, seal to seal is going to produce seals; however, if one or both of the seals carries what we call the blue factor or the dilute factor, then you may end up with seals, blues, and chocolates. Until you've bred your female, you can't always know whether she carries other factors, though you might make a calculated guess from her parentage.

Within the same litter, though, some will carry a dilute and some will not. It may even happen that your seal female or male will produce several litters of nothing but seals, with a seal, and then suddenly produce a blue. It's a bit like the roll of the dice. The same surprises are possible with almost any color combination.

Probably the owner of the stud you select can help you figure out what colors your kittens are likely to be.

REMEMBER, MALES HAVE JOWLS

Don't be disappointed if you go to see a potential stud and find that he just isn't as handsome and flashy as you had hoped. Older males tend to get stud jowls which make their heads look round, even though they may have quite a long muzzle. In addition, if they are seals or blues, they may have darkened. Usually they do. This has nothing to do with the kittens they can produce. If the cattery isn't heated, they may be wearing a winter coat which isn't the most beautiful.

Ask about what kittens they have produced. Maybe the owner has a photo of the male when he was younger. If he was shown, this may tell you something about his looks when he was younger. If he is a Grand Champion, you know that he was a handsome young male.

Disposition is another factor. If the owner is willing to let you pet and handle the stud in or out of his cage, this tells you something. Some studs get rather

neurotic after being caged over a period of time, but if you find this guy is sweet and affectionate, that's a very good sign.

You may hear the term "proven stud," and what this means is that the male cat has produced kittens. It's best to place an inexperienced queen with a proven stud or an inexperienced male with an experienced queen.

THE BEST ARRANGEMENT

Once in a blue moon, you'll encounter a situation in which a breeder is willing to bring his stud to your queens. If so, and you are set up to put them together without concern about his possible spraying, you may have a good deal. In general, though, you'll have to bring your girl to the male

"It may be difficult to be certain of the colors until the kittens are eight to twelve weeks old."

and, in most instances, this will involve her being put in a cage with him. If you've never caged her, you may hate the idea of it, but if she's in high heat, she really is thinking about only one thing. The cage is rather inconsequential. You mustn't humanize the situation. She'll be fine. Even a queen who starts out snapping and hissing usually ends up sleeping and eating with the male, and generally urging him on to greater and greater efforts long after he's lost interest.

Bringing her to him is usually the best because he is basically the one who has to perform, and he does it most easily on his home turf. In addition, a breeder who has studs may know best how to cope with getting the breeding accomplished. Your female may be so frightened by the situation that she'll go out of season for a day or two.

Sometimes the breeder may separate the two for a few hours and then put them back together, since it is rather nerve-wracking for both the stud and queen to be suddenly thrust together, strangers that they are. They may not get much sleep; she may not eat much.

FINANCES AND OTHER CONSIDERATIONS

In general, the owner of the stud will ask for a substantial fee for a successful breeding. Usually this fee will be due when you come back to pick up your queen, the breeder hopefully having witnessed (or heard) two or more breedings. He should also give you a pedigree of the male at this time.

Later, when the kittens are born, he should sign a litter registration for you to mail in to CFA or whatever association with which you are registering your kittens. There is no great rush on this, because you need to know their colors and sexes before you send in the registration. It may be difficult to be certain of the colors until the kittens are eight to twelve weeks old.

Most breeders will guarantee the breeding; that is, if you end up with no living kittens for whatever reason, the breeding can be repeated. Whether this is good for more than one repeat try varies. Some stud owners will take pity if you have only one living kitten and they may offer a second breeding. Some will even refund your stud fee if the breeding is attempted three times and still fails. This is a situation you need to talk about up front. If you are working with a guaranteed stud, the fault will probably lie with your queen. That's why some breeders may not want to go too far with guarantees. After all, he has worked as hard as he would have if the breeding had been successful—harder really, if he has repeated it.

SPECIAL DEALS

A stud owner who likes your queen may offer to reduce the stud fee for one or more kittens. Remember, though, that if he asks for best or best and second best or third best, you may be left with a bunch of pets. You need to think hard about what you're doing. What do you really want from the breeding?

If what you want is a top show cat, then pay your money and deal only with a breeder who'll let you keep all your kittens. Just think of what it costs to buy a top show cat. Why give one away?

You may be better off to keep your own litter and handle things on your own. Of course, the big "unless" is if you just plain don't have the money to pay for the breeding. You may have to wheel and deal, but don't be afraid to try to work something out if you have a nice female. It has been said that there are more "deals" than cash dealings in the cat fancy!

GETTING A CATTERY NAME

If you bought a registered kitten, it came with a cattery name, which was on the registration slip you filled out to complete the cat's

name. If you show or breed your cat, you'll want to have your own cattery name. You can obtain this by writing to the registry association of your choice. It will send you a form and all you have to do is send the required fee and the name you'd like to use. Registration charges vary from association to association. In addition, the permitted number of letters and spaces in a cat's full registered name may vary. When you sell a cat for show with your cattery name in front and the cat does well, this is very good publicity for your cattery.

Many cattery names are combinations of letters from the names of the husband and wife or partners who own the cattery, such as Del-Ri (Adelle and Richard Hathaway) and Tosa (Tony and Sandy Tanehsak). Others may be named for a special first Siamese, such as Waltur's, or you might prefer a made-up name, such as Nang Mao, Sea Shell, or Long n Lithe. Hopefully, whatever name you choose will turn out to be as good as your kittens.

Don't let the sweetly innocent expression of a Siamese kitten fool you. A kit can be as mischievous as it is angelic! These youngsters are from Teshari Cattery, owned by Terry and Shary Stracke.

CHAPTER

9

The Joys of Motherhood

"The mother will provide all the feeding and tender, loving care until the kittens are six weeks or so."

A healthy Siamese mother with a healthy litter of four or five kittens can be a total joy. The mother will provide all the feeding and tender, loving care until the kittens are six weeks or so. All you'll have to do is admire the kits and praise the mother.

Don't be afraid to handle the kittens after the first week. In fact, research suggests that kittens who have been handled by humans early on are probably less nervous and more curious and able to cope with a new environment than those simply left alone with their mother. This doesn't suggest, however, that the kittens should be a subject of interest and handling for friends who might happen to drop by. This can be frightening to the mother as well as the kittens.

HOW TO KNOW IF SHE'S PREGNANT

Don't decide that your queen wasn't bred just because she continues in season for three or four days after she comes home. If she was with the male only three or four days, even if she's bred, she may continue this behavior.

The first solid evidence of her pregnancy will occur at four to six weeks, when her nipples become noticeably pinker and larger. By then, you may also notice a fullness in the lower rib area and an increased, if not ravenous, appetite.

MORNING SICKNESS

This is not an unusual symptom of pregnancy and may occur early on, though most likely two weeks after breeding. It's not wise to make any drastic or unusual

change in her diet if she's having problems of this nature. Don't feed extra rations this soon because you've decided she's pregnant.

FEEDING THE MOTHER-TO-BE

There's no reason to change or supplement the diet of your pregnant Siamese during the first four weeks of her pregnancy. Quality, not quantity, should be your concern.

If you've been feeding her the recommended nutritious diet, supplemented with vitamins and minerals, you are safe to wait until about the fifth week of her pregnancy before you start upping her intake, starting then at about 20% and going on up to 50% by term.

Caru Chizu Adamma, who grew up to be a Champion (CFA) and Grand Champion (ACFA). This Chocolate Point is owned by Dayle Russell.

Be certain that you feed her high protein food—not too much dry or mushy stuff. Hopefully you haven't been feeding too much of this anyway. The best high protein food includes meat (fresh or canned), egg yolks, canned milk, and cheese.

Don't get over-zealous and fatten her up too much. This could make her delivery more difficult. What you want is muscle, not fat. You may decide to feed her three times a day, instead of two, especially if she looks "big." Pressure from the kittens could give her gas if she eats too much at one time.

VITAMIN AND MINERAL REQUIREMENTS

As with nutrition in general, you'll find many different opinions about just

A Blue Point female, Gr. Ch. Sin-Chiang Blu Velvet of De Vegas. Owners, Dan and Hanne Gauger.

which vitamins and minerals or other supplements are most important for your expectant Siamese.

Vitamin C and E advocates suggest that pregnant and lactating cats receive 1000 milligrams of vitamin C, in two equal helpings per day, and 100 IUs of vitamin E per day. Regular multi-vitamins don't provide these vitamins in these quantities.

Many well-known breeders have testified that this C and E program has resulted in healthy kittens from queens who previously had birthing problems, including resorptions, abortions, stillborns, malformations, and weak kittens.

CALCIUM AND VITAMIN D

Many breeders feed and recommend all sorts of special supplements for pregnant queens, most of them related to calcium, phosphorus, and vitamin D. Vitamin D is required for the absorption of the calcium and phosphorus. One common source for these minerals is a milk formula for kittens or canned evaporated milk (with or without the addition of 50% water).

Another sworn-by formula is brewer's yeast. Just be sure that you aren't already feeding a cat food that contains yeast. Too much could cause a stomach upset.

A lively group of Siamese and Colorpoint Shorthair kittens owned by Dr. Robert C. Koestler.

TOO MANY VITAMINS AND MINERALS?

Some breeders might warn you that feeding your pregnant queen too many supplemental vitamins and minerals during the last two or three weeks of her pregnancy could cause unusually large or heavy-boned kittens. They would, of course, be difficult for her to birth. The whole idea is untrue.

Genetic factors control the size of the kittens, though lack of proper nutrition could cause small, puny babies. In fact, during the last two weeks of gestation, the kittens are adding flesh and have little or no bone growth. The mother should be fed more protein and less starch and carbohydrates at this time.

A KITTENING PLACE

It's a good idea to prepare a cardboard box or other nesting place, such as a drawer or basket in a closet, a few days before delivery is expected. If you use a cardboard box, be sure it is clean—not one that could have contained produce sprayed for various assorted pests. This has been known to kill puppies.

If the box is high, it's a good idea to cut a notch in one side so that the mother can go in and out conveniently, even with her enlarged nipples. If possible, leave a flap on top to keep the box dark for the first few days. Shredded paper towels and/or newspapers are the best nesting material for birthing.

If other cats are around, you must place the box in a cage, private room, or closet so that the mother doesn't have to be concerned about protecting her babies. You may find that your sweet, placid girl has become a tiger once she has babies.

Leaving the box or nesting place until the last minute can be a grave error, because most mothers get a bit frantic about wanting their kittens to stay where they birthed them. Of course, there are those "nuts" who want to move them all over the place, but this is usually because they don't like the original place or they're just plain immature or having problems.

It's also wise to keep in mind that eventually you'll want her to litter train the kittens, and if they're free to run all over the place, she'll have a difficult time training them. All in all, a cage is the best idea. If she has them there, you won't have to worry about her dropping a kitten in a litter box or on the couch in the living room or whatever. She'll settle for having them in the box you've provided in the cage—hopefully. And she'll care for them there.

WHEN TO EXPECT THE KITTENS

A Siamese mother tends to have a longer gestation period than most other breeds. In general, she'll deliver around the 65th day from being bred but possibly as early as the 63rd day or as late as the 68th. Any days after the 68th become risky. It is best to take her to a veterinarian who can check out whether the kittens are alive or whether she has a problem. A vet can induce labor if she seems to have what is called "uterine inertia."

Another significant factor with these loving Siamese is that your queen won't want to have her kittens unless you are there to comfort and help her. You'll notice toward the last day or so that she'll stick to you like glue, following you from room to room. This doesn't mean that she won't be able to handle the situation. It's just that she loves you and wants you to be there in her hour of need.

My first show Siamese held off until the 68th day, although she had started labor earlier, waiting for me to get home from the hospital, where I'd had surgery. My coming home was based on the premise that I wouldn't get out of bed for several more days. Of course, she managed to turn all that around by proceeding to have her first kitten on the bed while I tried frantically to press her into the box.

Not only that, I once had

to run all over the house trying to find the kitten milk, a heating pad, and an appropriate container for the first kitten, which I was certain she had rejected. It never occurred to me that she might be too busy having other kittens to be bothered trying to nurse the first one. We were just about equally frantic. I put the first kitten in a shoe box with paper towels and kept it beside me on the bed. The mother went into her own box on the floor beside the bed. Later I found that my worries had been needless.

BIRTH IS IMMINENT

About 12 hours before the kittens are due, your queen will lie on her side. Her uterus will be contracting, the kittens being pressed into position for birth. Other usual signs are loss of appetite, although not always, and tearing things such as newspapers or paper towels in an effort to make a nest. If you've provided her with a box in a proper spot, she'll go there and rip up those papers and towels. As her delivery time approaches, her temperature will drop from between a normal 101 to 102 to 99 degrees. Although you may not want to hassle her at this time by taking her temperature, if you encounter problems, you may find this a significant indication of what's happening.

A clear-colored mucous

An old-type Siamese. Ch. Nicholas Jay of Rocat, a Seal Point male photographed at one year of age. Owner, Catherine Rowan.

In general, the Siamese possesses a pleasant temperament. This is Ch. Suzzi's Rembrandt of Velvet Paws, a Chocolate Point male owned by Doris and Bill Thoms.

discharge is another sign that the kittens will be arriving within 12 hours or so. This is normal, but if she should have a blackish, brownish, or greenish discharge, this is cause for alarm. Once her water breaks, you can be certain the kittens will soon start coming.

An inexperienced mother may seem very restless, licking herself, salivating, and going to the litter box over and over. A young queen with her first litter knows that something is about to happen, but she isn't sure what it is. I've had first mothers struggle to get out of the birthing box and try to run away even though labor has begun. Sometimes they just get plain panicky. They may

even birth a kitten in midair or throw it off in the litter box if you don't cage them or stick with them. It's not that they're unnatural mothers; it's just that they're inexperienced and frightened.

SUPPLIES TO HAVE AT HAND

In all likelihood your Siamese queen will take care of all the details of the birthing, but it's a good idea to be prepared for any possible problems. You'll want to keep her birthing box as clean as you can. A roll of paper towels, a grocery bag (for damp towels, etc.), a pair of not too sharp scissors that have been dipped in alcohol, a small extra box such as a shoe box, and a heating pad are the main things to have handy.

Most of us probably overreact. A friend told me about her queen's first litter. She had been advised to have sterilized scissors on hand and to wear plastic gloves if she assisted her queen at all. Well, the kittens started arriving a day earlier than she expected, and by the time she finished boiling the scissors and finding the gloves, her queen was lying there with five lovely kittens, wondering where in the dickens her "person" had gone, just when she needed her support.

THE SECOND STAGE OF LABOR

This is the serious stage. The kittens are placed ready to be born, and now the labor should begin. You'll notice the contractions as they ripple along the queen's body. She may pant and purr. Once this stage begins, though, you may still be in for a wait of an hour or so. Sometimes the female will stand and strain as if having a bowel movement, but usually she'll lie on her side or chest.

This is a good time to encourage and praise her. If it's her first litter, she really may be rather round-eyed and frightened. As the first kitten passes into the vaginal canal, she may strain very hard, maybe even press her feet on the side of the box or cry out.

Kittens will usually be delivered very neatly in their membranous sac, sort of like a goldfish in a plastic container. The sac may be ruptured before or during the delivery of the kitten or the mother may lick it off as the kitten comes out of the vulva. In any event, if the sac is not torn away within 30 seconds or so, you should help out. Probably the easiest way is to hold the kitten head downward and wipe off the sac with a paper towel, concentrating first on the mouth and head so that breathing can commence.

CUTTING THE CORD

Normally the placenta or afterbirth will come out along with the kitten and be attached by the navel cord. The mother will probably be instinctive enough to sever

Ch. Lur-O-Luv Lady Danae of Delian and her ten-day-old litter. Owners, Dolores and William Kennedy. A calm, quiet environment is important for a mother cat and her babies.

101

A nesting box should be kept as clean and as dry as possible. Enjoying a moment of family togetherness are Ch. Eldamar's Mirage of Tohpao and her kits. Owner, Brenda Conner.

the cord, but if not, you may want to help her. She could goof and bite it off too short, causing an umbilical hernia or unnecessary hemorrhaging. One of my Siamese bit off the tail of one of the kittens in her first litter in an attempt to sever the cord.

If you do decide to sever the cord yourself, which many Siamese breeders do, use scissors, preferably not too sharp, which have been boiled in water or soaked in alcohol. This comes closest to simulating the mother's teeth. Some people tie off the cord with thread or unwaxed dental floss about an inch from the kitten's stomach, after pinching the end of the cut cord or rolling it between their fingers to help stop bleeding.

CLEARING THE LUNGS

If the mother immediately begins to lick and tumble the kitten around, she'll probably do a good job of cleaning out any fluids in its

lungs left over from the amniotic sac. If you pick up the baby and hear a wheezing, it's best that you support its neck and thrust it head downward several times in order to clear out the mucous. If you see mucous around its nose and mouth, wipe it off with a tissue or paper towel.

DRYING A KITTEN

Probably more kittens are lost from chilling than any other cause. It's important to make sure the newborn babies are dried off and kept warm. If the mother works them over with her tongue and lets them start nursing right away, you shouldn't have any problems. Of course, if the room isn't warm or you're worried about a draft, it's best to put a heating pad under (not in) the cardboard birthing box, making sure you leave about a quarter or half of the box off the pad. That way, if it gets too warm, the kits can crawl into the unheated area. Too much heat could dehydrate them.

If the birthing is prolonged and the mother seems too tired or inexperienced to work with the kittens until she is finished with the entire litter, you may want not only to dry them off to stimulate circulation and help warm them up but also to set them off in a separate small container such as a shoe box. You can dry them with paper towels, old terry towels, or other rags you have around.

If, however, the mother seems to panic because she's lost one or more of her kittens, give her at least one back. It's best to keep her as calm as possible. Generally, she'll finish birthing in an hour or two.

BREECH BIRTHS

About 50 percent of the kittens will be in a breech position—hind feet first—and these births are more difficult for the mother. Sometimes you'll see only one foot protruding from the vaginal tract, and it may move in and out with the queen's contractions. You may see two feet, one foot doubled up, or only the tail.

It's a great temptation to grab hold and pull, but don't. You could easily damage the kitten or the uterus of the mother. Although it will take longer, she'll usually manage to birth the kitten without help from you or the veterinarian.

Other difficult delivery positions include an upside-down position with the kitten on its back; a kitten with its head twisted and coming out on its side; or an L-shaped position in which the kitten is at a right angle. Twins who share the same placenta may also be difficult for the queen to deliver. (Just think—if you

have identical twins that are of show quality, you could drive the judges crazy!)

Once you observe a delivery problem, check the time. If the kitten is trapped in the birth canal longer than 15 minutes or so, you should get the mother to the vet or attempt to help her yourself.

HELPING IN A DIFFICULT DELIVERY

The best early-on help is to stay calm and encourage the queen to keep bearing down. You can press her sides with your hands to stimulate contractions.

A demure Siamese kitten displaying all the charm of its breed.

By the way, if she's purring during all of this, you may come to accept the theory that purring is a product of pain as well as pleasure.

I have yet to help a queen by grasping a kitten and trying to pull it out. I've waited out the deliveries. Once it was nearly half an hour. At 3:30 a.m. I was throwing on some clothes to go to the emergency veterinary clinic when, presto, out came a nice healthy little kitten. And then promptly three more.

Other universal imponderables are, "Why does a queen with her first litter always have the first kitten in the breech position?" and "Why do the kittens always start arriving in the wee small hours of the morning or on holidays?"

Those who should know say that if time runs out, you can help your queen deliver a breech birth more directly. (This is advisable only if you feel you have the knowledge and/or experience to assist with a breech birth; otherwise, your veterinarian should be contacted.) First, you should sterilize your hands, of course. Then, using a paper towel or clean hand towel, pull gently on both of the kitten's legs as the queen labors, in a downward rotating motion. Do not pull on only the tail or only one foot. If only one

foot is visible, try to find the other foot inside the vaginal canal and work it loose and out with one finger. You may need to lubricate your finger with non-medicated vaseline or mineral oil in order to work it in more easily. This may also help slide the kitten out.

Don't get upset if one of the feet or both of the feet appear swollen or deformed after the kitten is delivered. This is mainly a temporary situation.

A CAESAREAN SECTION

If your queen can't deliver her own kittens, your veterinarian will undoubtedly suggest a Caesarean section. If time is on your side, this is a safe procedure. It may save not only the queen but all or most of the kittens. If all goes well, your queen will be awake and nursing her kittens within two hours.

The fact that your female has one Caesarean doesn't mean she'll have to go through this for future pregnancies. This will depend on why she needed the surgery in the first instance.

If she has what appears to be an ongoing problem , your veterinarian may suggest that you have her spayed immediately following the delivery. Once it's been determined that a queen has a birthing problem, it's foolish to continue to stress her by letting her go in and out of season.

A PROLONGED BIRTHING

It isn't unheard of that a queen will have one or more kittens on one day and finish up with one or more as long as 24 hours later. This gets scarey and could be dangerous. Some say it is because she was bred on two or three different days, though actually once ovulation begins, and this is within 24 hours, she is no longer receptive to mating. This doesn't mean, though, that she may not appear to remain in season. It is true that she could be bred by more than one male if she got outside and had access to them. She would then have a mixed litter.

RETAINED AFTERBIRTH (PLACENTA)

If the new mother seems nervous or sick, it could be because she didn't expel all of the placentas. You should try to watch for this if you are present when she has her kittens. Don't be surprised or disgusted if she eats one or more placentas. This is nature's way.

It's not essential that she eat the afterbirths, but they are believed to contain hormones that are beneficial to her health and well-being, as well as her milk production. What is essential is that no

placentas or unborn kittens remain in her uterus more than 24 hours.

Your veterinarian can give her a pituitary shot which will empty her uterus, relieving any fear of infection from either of these problems. This shot will also get her milk flowing if there is any problem in this area.

FOOD AND WATER

Your queen may get very hungry, thirsty, and tired in the process of birthing. Don't make her have to get out of her birthing box to eat or drink. Give her a little supplement of canned milk or water right in the box so that all she has to do is put her head down to lap it up. She may even like a bit of her favorite cat food or, as a special treat, some baby food.

AFTER SHE'S DONE

I usually do this one kitten too soon, and then have to start over, but when you think the litter is complete, you should remove all the wet materials and put in a

In general, kittens can start to be weaned between the ages of four to six weeks.

clean towel or rags. Try to make the box as warm and comfortable as possible. Don't use Great Aunt Emily's hand-embroidered tea towel just yet; your queen will have a slight bloody discharge for a few days. This is normal.

Once everyone is clean and happy, you and Mama can relax. She should be purring up a storm. She may have purred throughout the delivery. Most cats do. The kittens should be nursing. They'll sleep a lot too. They'll let you and their mother know when they're hungry by mewing. It's surprising how loud such tiny Siamese can meow!

Sexing a pair of Siamese kittens. The female is on the left; the male is on the right.

WHAT HAVE WE HERE?

It's difficult to tell what sex newborn kittens are, once the birthing is over and until the kittens are six weeks or

so. Usually the most aggressive ones at the nipples are the males, but, of course, you could have all males or all females.

The best way to determine the sex is to lift the kitten's tail and look beneath it. The female has a vertical slit-like opening just below the anus. This is the vulva. The male has a more circular opening quite a bit further down from the anus.

Don't decide you have a litter of albino kittens because you don't see any points or color on them. They're all born pure white, though you will see some variation in the degree of whiteness if you have seals and lilacs or chocolates. The dilutes are lighter. The color will begin to show around the edges of the ears and on the nose and tail in a couple of days. Even then, it may take up to six weeks to ascertain what color they are.

IF THE MOTHER REJECTS HER KITTENS

Most mother cats are very loving, protective mothers. They'll scarcely leave their kittens for the first few days after their birth. If the mother rejects one or more kittens, you can pretty much assume that something is wrong with the kitten or kittens or with the mother. A mother cat seems to know if a kitten is defective in some way and may refuse to care

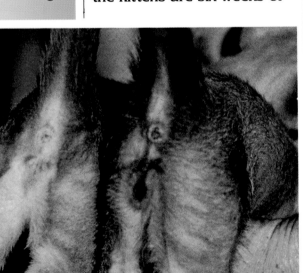

Tamago's Tank, a Blue Point male bred by Barb Fraizer and owned by Greg Elmore.

for it. She may even lie on it.

In a situation in which the mother is nervous and anxious to get away from the kittens, you may want to pack up her and the kittens and take them to a veterinarian. I had a mother and kits in such a situation, and when I took them to the vet he noticed immediately that the mother had no milk. Her breasts seemed enlarged, but she had nothing to feed her babies. A few pituitary shots brought down the milk and all was well.

Sometimes a young mother is just plain hyper and panicky for no particular reason. The vet might prescribe a tranquilizer in the hope of calming her down enough to enjoy her kittens. It's extremely important that the mother nurse them at least during the first 12 hours of their life so that they get colostrum, her first milk,

which contains antibodies that give the kittens resistance to diseases.

You may reform an indifferent or hysterical queen by simply holding her down on her side so that the kittens can nurse. She may decide she likes the kittens after all. You may need to try this several times during the first few days. If the kittens can't nurse, the mother's milk will dry up, and you'll have a litter of orphaned kittens.

It's an unpleasant thought, but a rare queen may show signs of cannibalism toward her kittens. If she seems aggressive and angry, she should be tranquilized and the kittens taken away until she settles down. A few queens find a first delivery traumatic and may blame the kittens if they felt pain. Often this will be a transitory situation, just remembrance of pain.

"The will to live is incredibly strong even in a tiny Siamese kitten, especially if it's healthy."

ORPHANED KITTENS

Don't give up on your kittens just because the mother does. If you can find another nursing cat, Siamese or not, and the owner is willing, you may be able to mix your kittens with the others and let that mother do the work. If you rub your hands on her own kittens and then on your own, she may be more likely to accept yours. It's also a good idea to present the kitten bottom side first. She may start licking it right away and will then accept the kitten.

IF YOU BECOME A SUBSTITUTE MOTHER

The will to live is incredibly strong even in a tiny Siamese kitten, especially if it's healthy. Although taking over as "Mama" to a litter of kittens is time-consuming and demanding, your attachment to that litter will probably be unusually strong. The kittens will be affectionate and people-oriented since they've looked to a human for all their needs from birth on.

Your first concern should be keeping them warm. Remember they have no mother to cuddle up against. You probably will need a heating pad under the box unless it's during the heat of summer.

The easiest and best milk to give them is a milk formula for kittens, which contains all the important nutrients kittens need. Since this formula is rather expensive, some breeders make up their own recipe consisting of one can of condensed milk, the same amount of boiling water, the yolk of one egg, and one tablespoon of light or dark corn syrup. Both the commercial milk formula or the homemade milk should be refrigerated but warmed slightly before feeding.

There are three or four possible methods of feeding. Probably the easiest for an amateur is a plastic eye dropper or a three-cc syringe. I've never had much luck with a baby-doll bottle or pet nursing kit. If you use an eye dropper or syringe, make certain the kitten is on its stomach, not its back, and open its mouth and insert the dropper or syringe at about a 45-degree angle. Be patient if the kitten tries to get away from the dropper. Once he gets a taste of the milk, he'll try to suckle. Don't rush him. He could choke. Feed him until he seems not to want anymore or until you notice that his abdomen is slightly enlarged. The amount will increase as the kitten gains strength and weight.

Inserting a tube through the kitten's mouth and directly down to the stomach is considered one of the best feeding methods, but it is a method your veterinarian would need to teach you.

Each kitten should be burped after each feeding. Hold him upright against your shoulder and pat his back. This will prevent stomach upsets.

Healthy kittens can probably do all right on four feedings a day. Sickly ones will need less milk more often. Don't wake the kittens up to feed them. It's best to wait until they begin to meow or seem restless. If you have a late evening feeding, you may even get to sleep through the night. If you can keep the kittens near your bed, you'll be able to monitor them more easily.

As substitute mother, you have one other task. Kittens eliminate through the licking of their mother, but if she isn't on hand, you'll have to use damp cotton balls or paper towels to rub their stomachs and anal area in order to stimulate excretion. Also, you may have to clean them up each time you feed them since they have no mother to perform this task. They will tend to soil their bedding with frequency, so you'll

Bright clear eyes are one important sign of good health. Check your pet's eyes regularly for any abnormalities.

have to pay attention and make certain they aren't lying on wet bedding.

THE EYES HAVE IT!

Siamese kittens usually open their eyes at five days old, a few days earlier than other breeds. If your kittens don't open their eyes about this time, you should examine them to make certain their eyes aren't stuck shut. This is not uncommon. Usually the queen licks their eyes to help open them, but if the eyes are infected, they won't open easily.

Don't try to force the eyes open. Sponge them gently with warm water on a cloth or paper towel. If the eyes open but continue to get stuck at intervals or, as is often the case, every morning, you may have to take the kittens to the veterinarian for a prescription of opthalmic ointment. You could try a boric acid eye ointment (available at the drug store), working it into the eyes two or three times a day, and if the condition is no more than a mild form of conjunctivitis, you may be able to clear it up. If there is pus in the eyes, press gently all around the eye sockets and wipe away the matter with a tissue or clean cloth.

It's imperative that you keep the eyes open and clear. If they become ulcerated, the cat's vision as well as the beauty of the eyes could be affected. In general, eye problems should be attended to by the veterinarian rather than your running the risk of complications.

After your kittens' eyes open, they still won't be able to focus or see much for a couple of weeks. The kittens will respond to your voice and vibrations of your footsteps from the floor. Gradually they'll begin to see shadows and forms and eventually they'll develop a very keen eyesight.

The deep sapphire blue of the Siamese cat's eyes is one of the most beautiful features of the breed. Crossbreeds, such as the Himalayan, have sacrificed intensity of eye color for Persian body type. The Balinese have only recently begun to have more intense eye color, mainly because they can be bred back to the Siamese without losing body type.

The only other cat with the same potential for the gorgeous, deep blue eye color as that of the Siamese is the white Oriental Shorthair, another hybrid of the Siamese.

If your Siamese have crossed eyes, they'll have to be considered pets, not possible show cats. Some prospective buyers seek the crossed eyes, but most people prefer normal eyes. If the eyes are extremely

crossed, you may find the poor kitten trying to jump on your lap and ending up back on the floor or somewhere off-side.

All of the reference books state that Siamese and other cats are color blind, perceiving only gradations of white-gray-black. I find this difficult to believe because, for example, I have Siamese who show a clear preference for a pink stuffed toy over a gold or blue stuffed toy, even though the toys are in all other ways identical.

Contrary to popular belief, cats and dogs are not natural enemies.

CHAPTER

10

Complications and Further Care

"It's during the last week of development that the kittens gain the little bit of fat and extra fur that will help them survive."

MISCARRIAGE

Now that we've considered the joys of motherhood, it's only fair to consider the problems involved in kittening. Fortunately these are often one-time problems. A queen can lose her kittens along the way, most often during the fifth week and most often on the 45th or 46th day. You may not be aware that this is happening.

The kittens may liquefy and be absorbed, leaving no clue that the pregnancy has terminated except that the mother stops gaining weight. She may pass them in the litter box or elsewhere and/or eat them, but since at this stage they are about the size of a grape, they may well go unnoticed, even if left in the box.

If there is vaginal bleeding, she'll keep herself licked clean. Queens are immaculate about this.

If you should notice vaginal bleeding at any time during her pregnancy, especially towards the end, you should rush her to the veterinarian. He may be able to administer hormones which will stop the impending miscarriage or premature birthing.

Kittens born earlier than a day or two don't have much chance of survival, especially Siamese, who are small normally and have such a small amount of fur to keep them warm. It's during the last week of development that the kittens gain the little bit of fat and extra fur that will help them survive.

Just because she miscarries once, there is no reason to conclude that your queen can't have a successful litter later on. You might want to have the vet

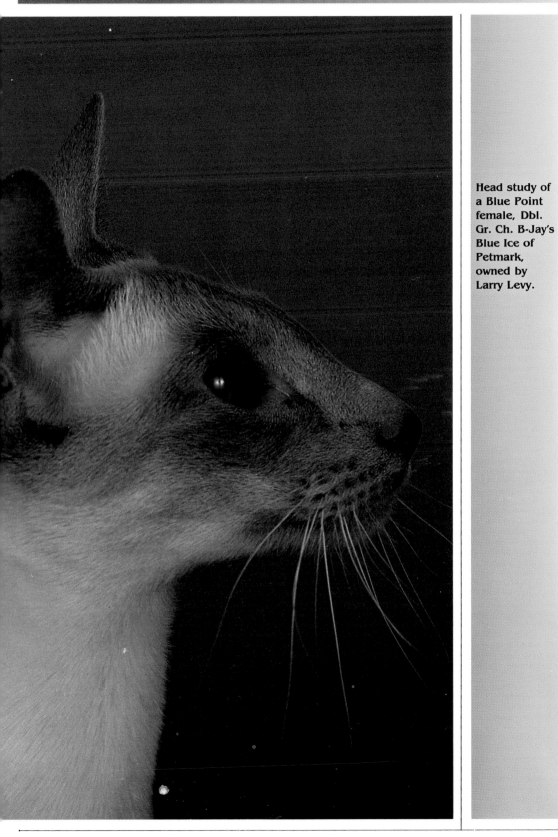

Head study of a Blue Point female, Dbl. Gr. Ch. B-Jay's Blue Ice of Petmark, owned by Larry Levy.

examine her for any observable cause of the miscarriage or to run some tests. For example, she could have a uterine infection.

Other possible causes of the miscarriage could be excessive jumping and exercise in the early stages of pregnancy, rough handling, injury, emotional problems or stress, poor nutrition, or a disease such as FIP or leukemia. Maybe your queen was just too immature. Some need to wait until two years or so.

It's possible that the fetuses weren't developing properly, and nature decided to be kind. You certainly wouldn't want abnormal kittens. Another possibility, rather unusual, is that the male with whom she was mated set up a lethal

factor with your female. Not much is known about this, but it seems to occur in a way similar to the Rh factor in humans.

FALSE PREGNANCY

This can happen after a sterile mating or for no apparent reason other than that the queen has been in season, usually several times, and gone unmated. Generally the physical cause is a growth on one or both ovaries.

All of the signs of a real pregnancy will be there, including an enlarged uterus, engorged breasts, eventually with milk production. The queen will want to make a nest and goes through all of the behaviors of an expectant mother, often feverishly. She may appear crazed and neurotic, carrying around toys and crying, but you should recognize that the problem is physical, not mental.

If there are other kittens or cats in the household, you may find her trying to adopt them and nurse them. She'll call out to them in a shrill voice as if they are all her own kittens.

Keep her away from other mother cats. She might try to steal their kittens or harm the mother in an attempt to take over.

The best solution to the problem is to breed her in her next season if she

Serve your Siamese his meals in a dish that is sturdy and easy to clean.

appears to be in good health and of normal weight. If this doesn't take, and she again has a false pregnancy, you may want to discuss alternatives with your veterinarian.

TIME FOR WEANING

If your kittens are healthy, you may be lucky enough to find them sharing their mother's food with no help whatsoever from you. This will most likely occur around six weeks.

In general, though, you'll need to encourage the kittens to eat and lap milk by putting some of the food or milk on your finger and onto or into their mouth. If they like it and are ready, you can repeat the process two or three times and then use your finger to guide the kitten's mouth down to the food. Some will catch on more quickly than others.

Mixing milk formula for kittens with a mild canned food, such as chicken, is an effective way to get them to start eating. They may also like cottage cheese or raw or cooked horse meat or hamburger.

LITTER BOX TRAINING

Once they start eating solid food, they'll need to be box-trained. Of course, if you have a mother on duty, she'll handle this quite smoothly. Two of the great unanswered questions of the universe are "What

makes a cat purr?" and "How does the mother cat box-train her babies?" It's almost impossible to catch a mom-cat putting the kittens in the litter box, but she must manage somehow, sometime. If you're the mom-cat substitute, you'll find that putting the kittens in a litter box after they've eaten is a good start to getting them interested. You might find it helps to let another cat use the box. Smell is very important to cats. It may take a few days, but soon you'll find your kittens prefer to use the litter box. They hate a dirty or damp bed.

Once you let them run out in the house or out of the cage (if they've been in one), you may experience a few setbacks on their potty training. Like children, they get so busy playing and running around that they may forget where the box is or fail to plan far enough ahead to make it to the box. You may want to move the box closer to where they

Three-week-old Blue Point Siamese and Oriental Shorthair kittens. Can you see the difference in their body colorations?

spend most of their time and then gradually edge it back to where you want it. Siamese are among the tidiest of breeds. Be sure to keep the litter box as clean as possible with young kittens, especially if several are using it, because if one has a bout with diarrhea or a stomach upset, they'll all get it if you let the box go.

VACCINATIONS

Your kittens will need their first shots at six to eight weeks. Your veterinarian can suggest which age he thinks is most effective. They already have immunity against the major cat diseases from their mother, but this is what is known as a "passive immunity." It may last from six to fourteen weeks. The problem is that if the kitten is vaccinated while still protected by this passive immunity, the vaccination will not be effective. That's why a second shot is given a month after the first, and often, a third, at four months.

Most veterinarians give a vaccination known as a "three in one." It provides protection against feline distemper, also known as feline panleukopenia or feline infectious enteritis, the most dreaded and fatal feline virus, and against the two most serious upper respiratory infections, rhinotracheitis and

calicivirus.

Make certain you keep records of the date of the shots since the kittens (then cats) will need a booster shot each year after the second or third shot.

Some veterinarians are recommending a rabies vaccination for cats at four months of age since the incidence of rabies is on the rise. If you plan to ship a kitten or cat to another state or country, you may find that you'll need not only a health certificate but a rabies shot. The rabies shot shouldn't be given until the kitten is four months old.

BY ALL MEANS, ENJOY YOUR KITTENS!

Siamese are naturally outgoing and affectionate, and the more attention and handling you give your kittens from four to six weeks on, the more sociable and well-adjusted they'll be. Starting at six weeks, kittens are curious and interested in people and the outside world. They should not be left in a cattery cage or a spare bedroom without affection or outside stimuli. This could result in fearful, neurotic kittens who'll never make satisfactory pets. Rough handling from children, other pets, or insensitive people could also adversely affect their attitude towards their environment.

What your kittens will

enjoy is a chance to run free and investigate the house. Introduce them to a scratching post, let them see where their food comes from and what's going on in your world, i.e., the TV, the stereo, the bathroom, the vacuum cleaner (which will undoubtedly send them off to hide the first few times), the dishwasher, and the like. They need to be exposed to all sorts of household sights, scents, and sounds. Keep an eye on them at first, but don't be overly concerned over every little jump or jerk they make. On the other hand, make sure you return them to their box (in their room or cage) for naptime if they are still only six to eight weeks or less. They do get worn out.

As you play with them, you'll begin to sort them out and know their personalities. No two are ever the same. Often there will be "The Mushroom," the lazy, easy-going one who'd rather sleep than exert himself. There will be the "Fun-Lover" who likes to chase and tease and attack

Owning two kittens is double the enjoyment, but not necessarily double the work. They can be companions to each other and their antics can be a constant source of amusement to you.

Long and lithe are two adjectives that aptly describe members of the Siamese breed. Elegantly posed for the camera is Gr. Ch. Tamago's Tori Oreo, a Chocolate Point female owned by Barbara Fraizer.

your hand if you move it back and forth. Later he'll want to play hide and seek. You may find the "Love Bug," who likes to look up from your lap into your eyes and flirt, and climb up, kiss and style your hair. There may be a "Prima Donna," who is already hyperactive, bossy and assertive about mealtime and special attention. There may be an aggressive one and a shy one and all variations in between. Their colors may have some bearing on how they behave, but even if you have an all-blue or all-seal or all-whatever litter, you are going to find fascinating differences in the personalities of each of the kittens.

It's fun just to watch them rough-house and tumble with each other. They'll run forward and attack and backward and retreat. They'll jump and turn sideways and arch their backs. They'll fight over territory at the top of a scratching post or hiss

and throw out their paws over a morsel of food. In fact, they'll already be carrying out all the behavioral strategems of cat culture with little or no help from you or another cat except their mother, if she is on the scene and still interested in her kittens.

Some mothers tend to lose interest after the kittens are weaned. They may even bite them gently but firmly on the head when they try to nurse or get attention. Other mothers will continue the nursing routine long after their milk is depleted. The breasts are like a pacifier for the kittens.

REGISTERING YOUR KITTENS

You don't have to register your kittens if you plan to sell them as pets, but if you think one or more of them might be of show quality, you'll need to register the litter. In order to do this, you must have the owner of the sire sign a litter registration form, and you must sign as owner of the dam. The registry association will require the registration numbers of sire and dam, number of kittens in litter, color, sex, and date of birth.

You'll register the kittens in the association in which their parents are registered. There is a fee for this, usually stated on the form available from the registry association. Fees vary from association to association.

The registration papers will be returned to the owner of the dam. If you have a cattery name and have put it on the form, the first name of each kitten will be that name. For example, if you chose "Tiki" as your cattery name, the registration form will show "Tiki" first in the spaces available for naming the kitten. No matter who

pedigree for your new kittens based on the two cats. You obviously can't sell a kitten with a pedigree if you can't come up with the papers. Pedigree forms are available from your registry association, from vendors at cat shows, pet stores, or mail order from ads in cat magazines.

Most kittens sold as pets don't come with a pedigree until the new owners give

If you are choosing a kitten solely for a pet, its disposition should be one of your first considerations.

buys the kitten, its first name will be "Tiki."

If the buyer has his own cattery, that name will appear as the last part of the kitten's name with an "of" in front of it. For example, Tiki Sweet Petunia of Ha-So.

You needn't rush to register your kittens. They can't be shown and shouldn't be sold until four months anyway. Do make sure you have the owner of the sire sign the litter registration form and give you a pedigree of his male. Without his pedigree, you can't make a mutual

proof of spaying or neutering. Otherwise there could be misunderstandings. Usually the new owners won't care about a pedigree anyway, though an occasional buyer may ask for it later, more or less for vanity's sake.

SELLING THE KITTENS

One of the most difficult things you may ever have to do is to sell your beautiful, loving, playful Siamese kittens. I've had friends advertise their kittens for sale and then tell potential buyers they were sold out

The point color of these kittens will darken as the youngsters mature.

when, in fact, they hadn't sold a one!

As the kittens grow older, you may reach a point at which you see it's best to find them a wonderful new home. It's just not practical for you to keep them all.

Keep a file of your buyers and make sure they know how to reach you if they have problems. It's a good idea to call them a month or so after they've bought the kitten to see how things are going. You might want to send birthday cards to your sold kittens over the years. You'd be surprised how many referrals this might bring, besides the obvious benefit of your keeping in touch with the cats' owners

in case of problems.

Often buyers lose touch with the person from whom they bought their cat. In case of divorce, illness, moving to another area, and other uprooting problems, they would probably call you, but if you don't keep them aware of how to reach you, they might just give the cat to the pound or an unsatisfactory home because they're under stress. You may not be eager to take a cat back after two or three years, but wouldn't you rather that than worry about what might happen to him? You can usually place the cat in a new home more readily than the original buyers can.

Standing on their hind legs is a natural ability for some cats. If you are interested in teaching your pet tricks, you might train it to stand on command. This agile kit is owned by Dr. Robert C. Koestler.

CHAPTER

11

To Show or Not to Show?

Showing cats becomes a "fever" for some exhibitors. If they have an outstanding cat, they may campaign it all over the country, looking for the big wins that could make their cat a regional or national winner. Others enjoy it greatly but show their cat in their own area at their convenience and hope for the best as far as wins go.

Visiting a local cat show is one way to find out if you might enjoy getting involved. You should buy a catalogue so that you'll get a clearer idea of what's going on. If your breed is the Siamese, you'll most enjoy seeing them being judged. This is also a good chance to evaluate whether your kitten or cat seems to measure up. The catalogue will include a schedule of judging for each breed in each of the rings. Most one-

day shows have four rings, each with its own judge.

Cats may win under one judge and not do well under another. Although each breed has its written standard with assigned point values for head, ears, tail, etc., no two judges will score a cat exactly the same. That's part of the fascination, and, occasionally, frustration.

Since there are numerous registration associations, all with slightly different standards and show rules, this book will deal only (and not thoroughly) with one well-known organization, the Cat Fanciers' Association. Information on the others is available through their national offices. Some exhibitors show in two or three different associations, especially if the associations are small and have only

CFA All-Breed Judge Donna Davis checking a Siamese's chin and jaw. If you are planning a show career for your cat, keep in mind that he should be tolerant of being handled.

occasional shows.

ENTERING A SHOW

If you decide you like the shows and your kitten or cat seems good enough to enter, you should get a flyer and official entry form and mail it in for the show in which you're interested. These forms are available for future shows at any show you might attend. Information on the dates and locations of many shows is printed in the major cat publications. Sometimes you'll see publicity in a local newspaper about a forthcoming cat show, but this is usually printed too late for you to enter. It is oriented toward getting spectators.

Cat shows are sponsored by cat clubs, some all-breed and some specialty clubs, which operate under the auspices of the various registering associations. Some require entries almost a month before the show; others who set up the entries and catalogue by computer can take last-minute entries (three or four days before the show).

Entry fees may vary. The entry clerk (EC in the listing) can answer your questions about the show or the filling in of the form. Once you enter a show or two, your name will go on a mailing list, at least locally, and you'll receive flyers about coming shows.

Your cat must be registered with the association holding the show. When you enter, you must include the cat's registration number. If you are entering a kitten (four to eight months), you can do so without the number, but your wins won't be scored.

A Seal Point kitten under the scrutiny of Betty O'Brien, CFA Judge. Some cats are not fazed by the rigors of a cat show; others may react somewhat nervously.

For some fanciers, having a cat that has achieved Grand Championship is a source of great personal satisfaction. Pictured is Gr. Ch. Sanlino Tina, a Seal Point female owned by Robert L. Molino, a CFA judge.

CFA-registered cats can be shown in most other associations once or twice before also registering them with that association. At eight months, your kitten becomes a cat and is then entered in the championship competition as an "Open." The goal now is for your cat to win six Winners' Ribbons, thus becoming a Champion.

Each Siamese competes only against like Siamese; that is, a Seal Point male "Open" competes only against other Seal Point male "Opens" and a Blue Point female "Open" competes only against other Blue Point female "Opens." It may happen that your cat will win automatically because it has no competition at the show, but judges can withhold what might appear to be an automatic win if the cat doesn't measure up to championship caliber in their opinions.

A visible kink in the tail or obvious poor health could be causes to withhold. Most judges will tell you quietly after the judging why they didn't hang the Winners' Ribbon on your cat.

The judging of the Siamese next comes down to the "Best of Color," with Opens, Champions, and Grand Champions all being judged against each other within the four color classes. The finale of the Siamese judging is the selection of Best of Breed, Second Best of Breed, and Best Champion. Any or all of these are likely to show up in the finals of that judge, where all the different breeds fight it out for the Ten Best Cats.

GROOMING FOR SHOW
Most Siamese exhibitors

groom their cats before a show, hoping to have them looking their very best. This goes beyond usual at-home upkeep, though, fortunately, Siamese (being short-coated) don't require the extensive grooming of such breeds as Persians. How far you want to go is an individual matter.

You can bathe your adult cat if you wish. Don't bother bathing a kitten. It will only remove the natural oils and make his coat seem fly-away. Even with an adult Siamese, it's advisable to bathe three or four days before the show, leaving time for the natural oils to return to the coat. Unless your cat has a flea problem, use a mild pet shampoo. Some contain brighteners to enhance the sparkle of your cat's coat, especially if it's a Blue Point. Washing also makes the coat feel silkier (if you don't remove all the oil).

If your cat's coat seems dry or is a bit longer than you might wish, try grooming products such as sprays which are anti-static and add protein or pH balance. There are many such products on the market.

Naturally, you'll make certain your Siamese is free of fleas and flea dirt before you take him to a show. The ears should be cleaned, as usual, with baby oil or mineral oil, making certain all the little crevices are free of wax or any evidence of ear mites.

You can brush your cat after you get to the show, but while still at home, you should remove any loose hair with a rubber brush. The coat will look much smoother and shinier. A final slicking with a chamois gives an added luster. You'll see Siamese exhibitors carrying their cats to the

Ideally, the coat of a Siamese should be smooth and shiny.

judging cages with cats and chamois in hand. By the way, a regular small chamois of the same type you'd use to dry a car is fine. Some pet shops sell chamois gloves, which are nice.

Make certain your cats' nails are clipped rather short, front and back. This is for the protection of the judges, and otherwise a judge could ask you to take the cat away, clip the nails closer, and return it. Of course, you may know your baby is docile and sweet and wouldn't hurt a fly, but most judges have been scratched or bitten a few times in their careers.

Some exhibitors trim all the hair from the inside of the ears of their Siamese to make the ears appear larger and more striking. A pair of snub-nosed scissors are safest to use. Special ear scissors are available at pet stores and often at the shows. Longer, random hairs can be trimmed from the cat's chin and the back of his front legs. The whole idea is to make the Siamese look *smooth*. Some breeders believe that the hair in the ears serves a purpose and refuse to trim it out. They seem to do their share of winning, also.

Incidentally, no matter how much you clean or trim, some cats have ear interiors that look absolutely white; others appear to have some

Gr. Ch. Terlin Misty Star, a Blue Point owned by Terry and Linda Little.

darker areas, which are not wax or dirt, but just the way the ear is colored. This is most frequently true of Seal Points.

FORBIDDEN GROOMING

Bathing with a shampoo that enhances the color of your Siamese is one thing, but to use tints or color rinses is another. This is forbidden by CFA rules. Any artificial coloring is taboo. The use of drugs such as tranquilizers to alter the natural actions of a cat is also forbidden.

Longer, stray hairs can be clipped to enhance the smoothness of the coat.

Gr. Ch. Singa Concertina, a Seal Point owned by Jeanne Singer.

By the way, just because your female is in season doesn't mean you can't show her. Some may stiffen their backs and act a little strange in the show ring, but this is something judges understand and will forgive.

PRACTICING FOR THE SHOW

If you've been to a show, you've seen the judges pick up a Siamese from behind, whirl him around, take a quick look, and plunk him down on the judging stand. Then the judge will pick him up again and raise him up, stretching the cat's body to its full length (hopefully) and sighting down the long, tubular body (again hopefully). Then he'll set just the back paws down on the judging stand.

Although most of this comes rather naturally to most Siamese, who are born show-offs (which is what is meant by a show personality), others ball up and refuse to be stretched or lift one of their hind legs when placed on the stand. If you go through the judging

VETTED SHOWS

A few shows are vetted, which means that as you check in, a veterinarian is on hand to examine your cat. If it should show signs of fleas, ear mites, ringworm or other fungus, runny nose or runny eyes, or a cold, he might refuse your entry into the show hall. Not many shows seem to be vetted anymore, but if your cat's health is questioned by the show management, you could be asked to take the cat to a veterinarian. Cats who are ill or who have been exposed to other sick cats should never be taken to a show. It's not fair to all the other cats and exhibitors there.

A Seal Point male, Gr. Ch. San-Li's Chao Fa of Cannoncats.

motions beforehand at home, accompanied by praise and petting, your Siamese will probably perform better in the ring. At least it won't all come as a frightening surprise in the hands of a stranger.

Since judges sometimes use a feather to get the cat's attention and help him show off to good advantage, you might want to try this at home also. They usually use a peacock or peacock-type feather. Occasionally a cat in the show ring acts totally indifferent to a feather, out of fright or the novelty of the situation. You want to give your Siamese every benefit possible before he hits the "big leagues."

CAGE DECORATIONS

When you visit a show, make certain you notice how the cages are done up. The sponsoring club furnishes each exhibitor with a wire cage for his cat, but it's up to the exhibitor to embellish this cage with curtains (usually on the inside or inside *and* outside) and some sort of rug and cozy bed for the cat. The curtains are not only decorative but they keep away drafts and give the cat a sense of security. He may not like the cat in the next cage if he sees him.

Most shows offer prizes for the best-decorated cages, sometimes to a specific theme, such as

According to the standard, the ears of a Siamese are strikingly large, pointed, and wide at the base.

Halloween, Christmas, the Olympics or whatever may be current. If you're artistic, you might enjoy getting involved in this.

For your first time out, though, you could settle for two single sheets and a towel or bathroom-type rug, plus some sort of pillow or bed. The sheets can be held on by the cage itself which has a lid which lifts. Also, assorted pieces of material, curtains, etc., can be used, attached to the top with curtain clips, clothes pins, or safety pins. Some

Judges are ever mindful of the breed standard as they evaluate each entrant in a show. Pictured is CFA Judge Kim Everett with a Siamese kitten.

Even if you do not plan a show career for your Siamese, you might find a cat show to be an interesting and educational experience. Pictured is Cathy Hummer, Siamese judge and breeder, examining a show entrant.

exhibitors drape a generous piece of material across the top of the cage.

The show flyer will state the cage size, which varies from one area to another, and by the company supplying the cages. You should bring your own litter pan (make it small) and bowls for food and water.

The club will provide litter and, sometimes, food samples, but don't count on the food. You probably won't want to feed your Siamese during the show, anyway, because he needs to be svelte to win. Most exhibitors feed only a *light* breakfast that day—cottage cheese, for example.

You'll want to bring your grooming tools for last-minute touches, especially your brush and chamois. If you have questions or concerns about any aspect of the show, call the entry clerk. He/she will know the answers and be glad to help you.

YOUR CAT'S NUMBER

Your kitten or cat will be assigned a number in the catalogue, and you'll be assigned a cage as you check in to the show. Check-in time will be indicated in the flyer. You'll be given your cat's number to put on your cage. Listen to hear that number called because that means your Siamese is about to be judged in one of the rings.

You'll carry him to the ring and put him in the cage with his number on it. The clerk who works with the judge will tell you when to take the cat back to its own cage. Try to cooperate by having your Siamese ready and getting it up for judging as soon as it's called. Otherwise the judging is delayed. You could miss the judging in one ring if you don't hear your call, though it will be repeated three times and sometimes more. The judging schedule in your catalogue should also help you anticipate when your cat may go up.

MAKING FRIENDS

One of the best things about the cat fancy is making new friends. Even if you're rather shy, you'll find that your mutual interest in cats will introduce you in an easy, natural way to many new people.

First you'll meet those benched around you, most of whom will be friendly and helpful, especially if you tell them you're a new exhibitor. Feel free to ask questions. They'll enjoy helping you.

You may find other Siamese exhibitors gravitating to you. They'll be interested in your Siamese and its breeding, especially if it's good. You'll also encounter the other Siamese people each time the breed is judged. You'll all be sitting or standing in front of the judging cages, waiting to see what happens. If you consult your catalogue or mark it as veteran exhibitors do, you'll soon see who owns which

A trio of Seal Point Siamese from an earlier decade.

cat, just as they'll know who you are before you even know they know.

CARRIERS

When you travel with your Siamese or take him to the vet or a show, you'll need to be sure he's in a safe carrier. Even if your cat cries while traveling in the car, it's best not to take him out of the carrier. He'll soon get used to traveling that way unless he has a special problem such as carsickness. Even so, taking your cat out of the carrier will do more harm than good because if he sees out the car window, he'll have an even stronger sense of motion. Also, there is always the danger that he'll get frightened and run under the brake or accelerator of your car.

Carriers come in a wide range of sizes and styles. The airlines require that a carrier be large enough that a pet can stand up and turn around as well as lie down and sit. This makes a good basis for choosing the right size for your Siamese, though if he's a kitten, you want to allow for growth.

You can, of course, find fancy and expensive carriers. These might impress some people at the shows, but the problem is that most of these carriers wouldn't be suitable for air travel or shipping.

There are also small airline carriers which tip and fit under a plane seat so that

Gr. Ch. Chez-Chats Wizard, a Blue Point male owned by Phil Morini.

Pet owners can choose pet furnishings that are harmonious with any given decor. These Chocolate Points are owned by Irene Brounstein.

your cat can stay on board with you in the passenger section instead of being stuck in the freight area. You have to make special arrangements with the airlines ahead of time and be the only pet owner in your compartment requesting such accommodations for this to work out. Of course, you have to pay air fare for the cat also, in passenger or freight.

Taking your Siamese to a show definitely involves using a carrier. There will be lots of other cats there, and you'd have a problem controlling your Siamese through check-in and then getting back to the car after the show without some sort of carrier. You will carry your cat "by hand" to the judging rings, however.

For comfort and warmth,

it's best to place a towel or some sort of bedding in the bottom of the carrier. Don't put the pillow or cuddle bed you plan to use at the show in the carrier until you're sure your Siamese travels well. Sometimes they miss using the litter box because of your rushing to the show or get sick and throw up.

WINNING BIG

Making your cat a Grand Champion isn't easy; in CFA, it takes 200 points, which means your Siamese, after becoming a Champion, must then win over 200 other Champions. If you see champagne being poured at a show, it's usually because somebody just Granded a cat. A cause for celebration! It's been known to happen in one large show, but most often it takes several shows to finish a cat.

A Chocolate Point Siamese owned by Norma Volpe.

yearbooks of the registry associations, you'll see many ads featuring top winning cats. These help to sell kittens to potential buyers who are looking for show-quality Siamese—or whatever breed is involved.

SHOWING ALTERS

Neutered males and spayed females, both known as alters, may be shown in what is designated as "Premiership" in most associations. The rules of competition are essentially the same as for "whole" cats although fewer points are required to achieve Grand Premier than Grand Champion. This is because the classes are much smaller than the regular Championship classes.

This is not to suggest that the Premiership competition is any less keen. It has become an increasingly popular way to show, especially for cat lovers who don't have the space or inclination to care for females in season or stud males. Many Siamese breeders prefer to sell their outstanding males to be shown as alters since it reflects well on their cattery when the male wins but doesn't lock him into the life of a caged animal.

CATS OF DISTINGUISHED MERIT

Cats registered in CFA are eligible to receive a

The next step up in CFA would be to achieve a regional or national win. This is based on the point total for a season. National winners may have been shown at many of the major shows in the country. Regional winners may have done some traveling, but they haven't necessarily been shown much outside their own region. No matter where the points are won, they count toward wins in the cat's home region.

These large wins enhance the reputation of the cattery from which the Siamese comes. If you look at the

Note the heavy-bodied appearance of these old-type Siamese. Contemporary Siamese have a svelte, elongated look.

Certificate of Distinguished Merit. Any male who sires fifteen or more Grand Champions and/or Grand Premiers, and any female who is the mother of five Grand Champions and/or Grand Premiers, qualifies. These cats will then have the suffix "D.M." added to their names in addition to any prefix titles.

CHAPTER

12

About the CFA Siamese Show Standard

THE 1965-1966 REVISION

Very few changes have been made in the CFA Siamese Show Standard since it was revised between 1965 and 1966 by some of the top Siamese breeders in the nation. The fact that the standard has remained almost constant speaks well for these breeders and the breed. It would be difficult to try to breed cats to meet a standard that was constantly changing. It's difficult enough to come near an existing standard with any regularity.

At the time the committee presented this amended standard to the board, it was emphasized that the standard can't apply to any living cat, that it should "serve as a guide to the future improvement of the breed."

"It would be difficult to try to breed cats to meet a standard that was constantly changing."

STANDARD FOR COLORPOINTS AND ORIENTALS

The CFA standard for Colorpoint Shorthairs uses exactly the same point scores as the Siamese standard and uses almost exactly the same description of type. The only difference is in allowable colors.

The Oriental Shorthair standard is also very similar to that of the Siamese, though, of course, eye color and body color differ greatly.

THE PHILOSOPHY BEHIND A STANDARD

At the time the new standard was presented to the CFA Board in the 1965-1966 season, Mrs. Jeanne Singer (Singa Siamese), chairman of the Breed Committee, wrote a preface

Naturally, you'll want your Siamese to look its best for a show—bright-eyed, healthy, and well groomed.

which she simply titled "Basic Thinking About the Siamese Standard."

This preface was so appreciated by the CFA Board members that it was edited to broaden its scope, removing all direct references to Siamese, and used as a preface to the CFA book of standards for all the breeds.

Following is Jeanne Singer's original preface with specific references to the Siamese still intact. No novice breeder or any breeder, for that matter, could do better than to internalize the philosophy expressed here and strive towards producing the most beautiful, healthy, harmonious Siamese possible. This is what breeding should be about!

BASIC THINKING ABOUT THE SIAMESE STANDARD

I'd like to start some fresh thinking about standards. What is a standard? It is not a cat. A standard is an abstract aesthetic ideal. The realization of a good standard would result in a work of art, or at the very least, an object possessing artistic unity. Artistic unity requires that individual parts be in harmony with one another; that they possess balance and proportion; that together they enhance each other and strengthen the whole. A good work of art has its own inner logic. There is a feeling of inevitability and rightness about each detail. With a standard we aim at some satisfying visual shape which possesses a certain style. Style, too, implies an inner harmony and consistency between the parts. In the realm of aesthetics the whole is really greater than the sum of its parts, but each part enhances or detracts from the whole.

Is the Siamese standard a good standard? Would its

An old-type Siamese. If he is left unattended outdoors, your cat's natural curiosity could get the best of him and thus put him in any number of potentially dangerous situations.

Silvern's Angel of Bahn Yindee, a Chocolate Point, and her mother, a Lilac Point.

realization possess aesthetic or artistic validity? I say yes. It can be reduced to one unified concept of an elegant, streamlined object characterized by long tapering lines. The style is refined and graceful. It aims at a total effect of distinctively stylized beauty. I say a cat which lived up to the basic intentions of the Siamese standard would be beautiful by any standard.

How often we have heard this remark applied to some exquisite Siamese, "Why it looks like a statue!" This is an unconscious acknowledgment that a good Siamese resembles a work of art.

Nothing grotesque or distorted or ugly is implicit in the standard. Why then do some winning Siamese look ugly or distorted? Because they violate in some way the basic intent of the standard. Too much emphasis on individual parts can obliterate the total concept. A cat can have individual "good" features yet not fullfill the ideal of the standard.

In a poor or amateurish work of art, some parts clash or cannot be harmonized with other parts. There can be much brilliance coupled with abysmal weakness. Artistic unity is impaired or absent.

I think if you analyze any Siamese who appears "ugly," you will discover that some feature or combination of features does not blend in well, or abruptly interferes, with the basic pattern of lines. In other words, something clashes with the style.

Excessive exaggeration, distortion, or contradictory parts creates a grotesque instead of a pleasing image. Intentionally distorted and exaggerated features can also create a ludicrous or comic effect. Such is the nature of caricature or cartooning. However, the Siamese standard does not imply intentional distortion of any one part at the expense of another. The implication of the Siamese standard is that all lines are long and slender, tapering off to points—tail, ears, head, feet—and the effect of these tapering lines is a creature both dainty and svelte. Hardly grotesque! A blunt, square muzzle, round short ears, large square feet, for example, would contradict the total aesthetic image. There is a delicate balance between that which enhances the style and that which distorts.

The standard does not describe a living cat. It is an artistic ideal which is never completely attained on one specimen. We merely try to approach the ideal, always aware that perfection lies beyond our grasp. This is what keeps us inspired, much like an artist.

Suppose we work backwards on the standard. Instead of starting with details and adding them together to arrive at a whole, let's start with our basic style and evolve the details from

the style. You will see that the component parts cannot be slung together in an arbitrary fashion. You do not have the choice of any shaped head or any shaped tail. You must choose the shape which best enhances the basic pattern of slender, elongated, tapering lines and daintiness. A large round massive head on a long slender neck would be obviously grotesque—or a thick blunt tail extending from a long graceful back. The long wedge-shaped head is, thus, the most logical shape for our style. It tapers down to a fine muzzle suggesting a point—balancing the long whip tail which also tapers away to a point on the other end. It is also logical for the lines of the head wedge to sweep up to the tips of the pointed ears. If the line is thrown off by a faulty earset, our pattern is interrupted and weakened. The large pointed ears are necessary to balance the length of the wedge beneath them. The long slim legs must, logically, taper down to dainty feet. The eyes are compelled to slant to enhance the wedge effect of the head. And, of course, the body must be long and fine or the whole concept will be nullified.

So you see, there is inner logic in the Siamese standard. We cannot alter the standard, our "ideal" of

"Excessive exaggeration, distortion, or contradictory parts creates a grotesque instead of a pleasing image."

Older style Siamese are sometimes referred to as being "apple-headed," a term that refers to the pronounced roundness of their heads.

beauty, to accommodate every odd variation that nature produces.

We must heed nature, though, as far as healthy functioning is concerned. Is the Siamese standard unnatural? Does it work against the best interests of nature? Most emphatically, no. In fact the wild species, such as lions, tigers, leopards, favor our elongated style. What beautiful long flat profiles those lions have! What long sleek bodies those leopards! And what cat has longer legs than the cheetah?

In refining our standard, we must avoid any feature which could look gross or coarse. All features, aside from being elongated, must stay within the concept of dainty and svelte. I'm reminded of some massive bulldog chins that have been shown lately with much pride. They would look great on Persians! True, they are not receding, but are certainly gross exaggerations of the Siamese ideal. They look ugly and out of place on a dainty cat. Heads, too, can look very coarse and ugly even if they are long. Length alone does not make a Siamese head. Shape and proportion are equally important.

The standard can or should set down to the last millimeter of a whisker a scientifically exact diagram of a cat. Nature never produces exact replicas anyway. The standard is an objective and artistic guide to a judge's own good taste and educated sense of proportion. In like manner a composer sets down his notes, tempo, dynamics, and phrasing, as a guide to the interpretive musician, but must rely on the musician's own sensitivity and knowledge of style to make the music live.

A cat is a living, breathing, moving being that must be observed as such—not an inanimate piece of machinery or a frozen corpse. Certain things a good musician would never do—such as interpret slow for fast or loud for soft. Likewise a

The historical background of the Siamese is as unique as the breed itself. Pictured is a three-month-old Blue Point Siamese owned by Susan P. Tilton.

good judge could never interpret coarse for fine or short for long, though these terms be merely relative and not absolute. Ask yourself, how long is long or how tall is tall? This is where the "art" of interpretation operates.

Cats cannot be computerized. Who would really want that? Just imagine the dubious thrill of sending in your cat's measurements on one of those "do not fold, staple or bend" cards and having the winner spewed out by an electronic brain!

If the various parts of a cat are harmoniously balanced and complement each other well, the whole will be greater than the sum of its parts. The total will be a beautiful cat. We should consider this to be the ultimate discipline of our Siamese standard.

Colorpoint Shorthairs have the same general conformation as Siamese.

CHAPTER

13

Starting a Cattery

Once you've become hooked on showing or breeding Siamese cats, you'll find you want not only a cattery name but a cattery in the total sense. At the least, you'll be thinking of one or more breeding females and maybe your own stud. Determined as you may be, you should stop to realize that a cattery is a time-consuming, expensive, sometimes frustrating, but always fascinating hobby. It can become a small business, though most breeders hardly break even, much less show a profit.

CHECK ON ZONING

One of your first concerns should be whether the zoning in your city or neighborhood allows you to have more than two or three cats on the premises. If not, you may find yourself in trouble with local animal control agencies if you exceed this limit. The authorities won't usually bother you unless your neighbors complain, but, of course, it's much better if you live in an area in which your cattery can be licensed by the city or county. Otherwise the day may come when a knock at the door throws you into the trauma of getting rid of most of your cats.

If you've invested in expensive stock, cages, etc., you'll feel very stuck. Siamese queens are so noisy when they're in season that it's virtually impossible not to bother your neighbors if you live in a close residential area. Breeders in some cities are concerned about advertising kittens for sale because an animal control person might call, posing as a potential

buyer. Areas zoned for cats are similar to those zoned for dog kennels and horse stables. They tend to be suburban or rural, and the houses are further apart.

For the most part, though, small breeders who keep their cats clean and well-contained don't encounter any real problems.

PLAN CAREFULLY

If possible, don't just sort of let your cattery happen; plan carefully and know what's involved and what your goals are.

For example, don't build your cattery around a mediocre queen because she is well-loved at home. It will take a very exceptional male to correct her flaws, and meanwhile you're spending your money and spinning your wheels.

Keep your mediocre queen and enjoy her. Later you may be able to use her as an outcross, but what you really should do if you're serious about breeding is to buy the best queen available from a trustworthy breeder. She may be expensive, but you're about to invest considerable amounts in cages, stud fees, entry fees, food, vet bills, advertising, etc., in order to start a cattery.

Every time you go to a show, study the cats being shown. Notice which lines appeal to you. To be an important cattery in the future, you'll need to develop a "look." This takes time, of course, but your dream should be that some day knowledgeable breeders

Chanthara Paddington Bear Quinella, owned by Jim and Sue Graber, reflects the beauty and elegance that have attracted admiration for the breed.

make a silk purse out of a sow's ear, but there is no insurance. Every breeding, even between the same two cats, produces somewhat different kittens. That's part of the fascination, but usually you aren't going to find a fabulous potential Grand amongst a boxful of pets.

A KITTENING CAGE

Even if you don't own a male, you'll find that a small cage will be handy if you breed your female. Often you can keep a kittening cage in your bedroom where your queen will feel close enough to you not to object to being contained. Most pet stores or vendors at cat shows sell collapsible wire or plasticized-wire cages. Dimensions of approximately 2 ft. wide by 4 ft. long by 2 ft. high are adequate for a kittening cage.

If you allow your pregnant queen to run free too late into her pregnancy, she could abort her kittens by jumping and rough-housing. If you cage her a couple of weeks before the kittens are due or at least cage her part of the time during that period, she'll adapt much better than if you wait until she births the babies.

Once the kittens are born, you can let the mother in and out as she wishes, but probably for the first day or

will look at your kittens or cats and say, "Oh, yes, that's a 'such and such cattery' cat." The only way to achieve this is to start visualizing what you like most and to spend the money to go after the cats who might be able to achieve it for you.

The joy of breeding is to produce the best kittens possible, not to repeat the same mistakes and weaknesses over and over. Buy a top female, show her to Grand Champion, and then breed her to an outstanding male. All too many small breeders go on year after year showing the same mediocre stock, dreaming of the big win but never setting up the right situation to provide it.

Breeding mediocre to mediocre tends to produce mediocre. Breeding mediocre to Grand Champion quality may or may not produce a winning Siamese. As mentioned, linebreeding may help you two, she'll stick tight with her litter. If you aren't home during the day, you can even open the top of the cage so that she can go in and out as she wishes during the first four weeks or so. The kittens will be too young to crawl out. Be careful, though, if you have other cats in the house. She won't want them bothering her babies in any way, shape, or form!

A small cage is also useful if you need to get one or two cats out of the way while you're entertaining dinner guests or working around the house. Putting the cats off in another room behind a closed door works out fine with some Siamese, but others (maybe more spoiled) may fling themselves at the door, scratch the door itself, or, even worse, scratch up the carpeting near the door. A cage eliminates the problem. If your Siamese objects to a cage, you might try giving him a little treat each time you put him in the cage.

MOVING ON UP

Going beyond a cage or two in the house, you need to look very seriously at what sort of accommodations you're prepared to provide for your cats. How much space do you have? How much can you afford to spend? What would be your maximum number of cats?

Some breeders may partition off part of their basement for a cattery, assuming the area has windows for sunlight. Then they add heat and cages. Other breeders may adapt garages or add on an enclosed, covered patio to the side of the house or garage.

Spare rooms within the house can be utilized, though this will require extra effort in terms of odor and sound control. Of course, any out-building can be adapted or out-buildings can be created, though this is an expensive way to go. The most important considerations will be sunshine, fresh air, spaciousness, heat for cold weather, and, possibly, air conditioning for hot weather. Siamese aren't fond of air conditioning unless temperatures are really unbearably high.

A trio of Siamese relaxing in their bed. Sometimes breeders get so attached to a litter that they end up keeping more cats than originally planned for.

Outdoor exercise cages, such as dog kennels but with a lid, are a wonderful bonanza for caged cats. These can also be built out of two-by-fours and chicken wire. If they're adjacent to the cattery, it's nice if you have access to the cages through a door or window. In warmer climates some cats adapt to living out-of-doors all year long—with, of course, a warm house inside the cage and a tarp overhead to keep out the rain. Their coats will reflect the weather, getting heavier and possibly darker in winter and lighter in summer. You wouldn't want to leave a show cat outside since his coat would defeat him in the ring.

LARGER CAGES

Within your cattery, you'll need to fabricate your own cages or buy cages which can be brought in.

Ideally, the stud or studs should have floor to ceiling cages since they mainly live in their cages. If you have outdoor runs for them, this could change their needs somewhat. Queens can tolerate smaller cages because they're usually allowed to run out and play during at least part of the day.

If you have more than one stud, you may discover that letting even one run out within the cattery can foment trouble. He may rush at the cage of the other stud and become quite difficult to handle. He may also spray all over everything including the other stud in his cage.

KEEPING THINGS CLEAN

No matter how you set up your cattery, make your number one priority ease of cleaning. The more cats you have, the more crucial cleanliness becomes.

The cages should have surfaces of formica, linoleum, semi-gloss, or gloss enamel (preferably coated with urethane) so that they can be easily scrubbed. Avoid the tile squares. Siamese studs who are sprayers will manage to spray their urine between the little cracks. You'll wonder why no matter how hard you clean, the cage still smells of male. Linoleum is a better way to go, especially if you can cove it along the sides.

There are various effective disinfectant scrubs available including forms of tamed iodine and bleach. Ammonia-based products are good cleaners but tend to produce an odor so urine-like that they encourage spraying. A combination of bleach and PVP iodine, each 1/32 to water, appears to be optimal for most viruses.

Daily scrubbing is almost a must with spraying males and sometimes spraying females. Your cats will thank you for this daily attention.

Litter boxes should be not only changed but scrubbed out with a disinfectant every couple of days.

DON'T GO OVERBOARD

Making your cattery a veritable doll house may look cute for a month or so, but if you have cats who run out of their cages during the day, you'll soon find your doll house has become a disaster area. Rosettes and ribbons from shows (even if hung high on the wall) will be quickly shredded. Siamese often jump from cage top to cage top or up to and from any piece of furniture in the room. They'll pull off the paper towels and carry them all over the cattery. They'll tip over the waste can. They'll get into any storage cabinets you may have unless they're cat-proof . . . Siamese-proof, that is. They may spray (females too, if they're in heat) on any tables, furniture or even a radio available in the area.

I don't mean to sound negative toward our beloved Siamese, but I do feel a twinge of jealousy when, for example, a breeder of Exotic Shorthairs says, "Oh, we solved our problem of too many studs. We built a nice new cage and all six of them live in it with no problems."

Well, we make our choices. Too many Siamese have been known to provoke a nervous breakdown.

That's why the proper cattery setup can be extremely important.

BEWARE OF ELECTRICAL OUTLETS

Be especially careful of electrical cords and appliances. Not only might your cats bite through the cords and injure themselves (severely), but if they spray into outlets, the urine may cause an electrical short or a cycling with a flash of flames which could lead to a fire. Using space heaters which have to be plugged in is a definite danger with Siamese on the loose, even though the heater may be guaranteed to shut off if tipped over. What if a cat sprays into it or throws paper plates or paper towels onto it?

If all your cats are kept in cages, then you may be able to keep the cattery looking spiffy and use space heaters, etc., but it's all

Your pet's bedding items should be cleaned periodically.

Siamese are sociable and affectionate in nature.

something of a trade-off. How much freedom do you want to give to your cats? Or take from your cats? How important is it to keep them enclosed? The real solution lies in keeping your cat population small and your cages large.

AIR FLOW

Research veterinarians are stressing more and more that the best control of diseases is a constant exchange of fresh air in your cattery; that is, open windows which allow 10-15 air exchanges per hour. This is by far more important than warmth in the control of upper respiratory diseases.

High humidity is another potential danger, according to Dr. Frederic Scott of Cornell University. Not only can it lead to viral infections but fungal problems as well.

THE IDEAL CATTERY

Most of us will never have the money it takes to create

what we will come to conceive of as our dream cattery. For example, I'd like one with a refrigerator, a sink, an electric can opener, heat and air conditioning, storage cabinets for food, grooming supplies, and first aid kit. The floor to ceiling cages would be on wheels and have removable partitions for adaptability to all sorts of different situations.

Of course, there would be lots of windows to let in the sunshine, an access from the cattery room to wonderful outdoor runs. Then I'd like space for a desk and file case (a small office—let's face it) with a telephone where I could carry out my cat business and hold a couple of Siamese on my lap while I talked. And, oh, a display case for rosettes, ribbons, and trophies would be nice. A grooming table would be nice and maybe a separate area for cats who aren't feeling up to par, and, oh, well, we mustn't get carried away! Maybe we could add a couch and just live there. How about that?

ESTABLISHING AN IDENTITY

Starting a cattery is not unlike establishing any business. You'll want other "cat people," judges, and potential buyers to know who you are and to appreciate your Siamese.

Your cats should always be

immaculately groomed. Your cage decorations should not only be tasteful but clean and well-pressed. Your carriers should be well-scrubbed.

Attractive business cards are also a big plus. I've had many calls for kittens months after a show from people who just happened to walk by and pick up one of my cards. I've sometimes cringed as little kids grabbed a handful of cards, only to get a phone call weeks later from a mother who was interested in buying a kitten just like "that one of yours Joey saw at the show."

YOUR CATTERY AS A TAX DEDUCTION

Once you start handling your cattery as a small business, you're probably eligible to use it as a state and federal income tax deduction. To start off saying "deduction" may sound negative, but, as mentioned, very few cat breeders make a profit. Occasionally someone will run lucky and come out $200 or so ahead, but it's a difficult feat.

Using the cattery as a tax deduction is certainly fair if you keep accurate and complete records and give an honest accounting. Some dog and cat breeders believe that if you go beyond five years without making a profit, the IRS will

automatically "get on your case." This isn't necessarily true. What they may do at some point is to question whether your cattery is a business or a hobby.

You'll be treating your cattery as a business. If you're licensed and have a separate bank account, that's all to the good. Even so, if your cattery is registered with an association, and if you sell one or more kittens per year or take in stud fees, you can then offset this income with your cattery expenses.

An eight-week-old Siamese displaying his already straight profile. Owner, Brenda Conner.

CHAPTER

14

Naming Your Kittens

ENDLESS POSSIBILITIES

Naming kittens can be an intriguing easy-chair pastime, or you may find yourself looking everywhere for names . . . on freeway signs, street signs, parks, towns, nations, plants, trees, etc.

Some breeders name all of the kittens in a litter with an overall theme, such as Broadway shows: Evita, Oliver, Hello Dolly, and Funny Lady. Others name only the kittens they intend to keep for themselves. They may wait to name them until their personalities suggest really suitable names. Kittens can be shown under any call name until actually registered.

If you do decide to name whole litters, the names should be kept rather short because they'll eventually include not only your cattery name and the kitten's name

but also the cattery name of the buyer. (CFA permits only 35 letters and spaces for all three of these names.) Also some potential buyers may already have chosen a name they'd like to use for their new kitten. If you've named the kitten, they'll be stuck with that name.

The possibilities for names seem almost endless: movie titles, vocal groups, book titles, songs, TV shows, beverages, flowers, mythological figures, and so on. Thus we come across a variety of names at cat shows: Flashdancer, Brandy Alexandra, Boy Howdy, Jeremiah, Amazing Grace, Kan Kan, Sheba, Hill Street, Name That Tune, Thriller, The Right Stuff, Pandora, Maximillian, Second Hand Rose, Broadway Joe, Shogun, Miles Davis, Kiss My Grits, Gang Buster, Elmer

"Kittens can be shown under any call name until actually registered."

An old-type Siamese. Ch. Suzzi's Rembrandt of Velvet Paws, a Chocolate Point owned by Bill and Doris Thoms. Notice that for a mature cat (eight years) Rembrandt's point color has remained restricted to his extremities.

Fudd, Boca Grande, First Lady, My Main Man, and Mae West.

The color of a Siamese is sometimes included or implied by such names as Serenade in Blue, Blue Minstrel, and Blue Max (Blues); Sealebrity, Sealia, and Sealebration (Seals); Lotta Lilac, Pin-Kee, The Pink Panther, Robert Frost

A Siamese enjoying a favorite feline pastime—scratching its claws. In your home, be sure to provide a scratching post for your cat, or he may select inappropriate objects, such as curtains and rugs, for this activity.

(Lilac Points are called Frost Points in Great Britain); Mocha Rocha, Chips Ahoy, and Famous Amos (chocolates).

There are cattery owners who stick with one theme for all their Siamese. Others enjoy puns and humor, even at the cat's expense. Cat registry associations do, however, insist that breeders "keep it clean."

Interestingly, what you name your kitten may not be what you end up calling it at home. Cats often have show names which are completely different from their "call" names.

TRADITIONAL THAI NAMES

You may want to use traditional Thai names for your kittens. They seem to fit very well. The following names are suggested by Anthony Tanehsak, a native of Bangkok, Thailand, who is now a United States citizen. He was active in breeding and showing Siamese cats for ten years in the United States.

Colors:

Seal: Si-Nam-Tan-Mai (M or F)

Blue: Si-Far (M or F)

Chocolate: Si-Nam-Tan (M or F)

Lilac: Si-Khoa-Toa (M or F)

Precious Jewel: Keow-Manee (F)

Noble: Dee-Lert (M or F)

Dancer: Nak-Tan-Rum (M or F)

Beautiful: Sue-Ngarm (F)

Tiger: Sue-Dow (M)

Lion: Sin-To (M)

Free Spirit: Isara-Parb (M or F)

Happy: Suk-Sarn (M or F)

Princess: Choa-Ying (F)

Prince: Choa-Chai (M)

Beloved: Ti-Ruk-Ying (M or F)

White Lotus: Bua-Khoa (F)

Star: Dow (M or F)

Moonlight: Sang-Chan (F)

Royal: Sue-Sak (M or F)

Mystical (or pure): Borisuk (F)

Sweetheart: Yod-Rak (F)

Naughty: Sook-Son (M or F)

Lively: Ra-Lern (M or F)

Cat: Mao (M or F)

Sapphire: Phai-Lin (M or F)

True Friend: Phuen-Tae (M)

Orchid: Dok-Kua-Mai (F)

Jasmine: Dok-Mari (F)

Pearl: Khai-Muk (M or F)

Diamond: Petch (M or F)

Precious: Na-Ruk-Ying (F)

Agate: Mora (M or F)
Emerald: Morakot (F)
Ruby: Tup-Tim (F)
Garnet: Komain (M or F)
Amber: Am-Phun (M)
Jet (Blue): Nin-Far (M)
Jet (Black): Nin-Dum (M)
Zircon: Pa-Thai (F)
Cat's-Eye Stone: Petch-Ta-Mao (M)
Real Gold: Thon-Tae (M)
Gold: Thon-Karm (M or F)
Best Sky: Lert-Far (M)
Splash (Water): Tomm-Tamm (M)
Most Beautiful: San-Ngarm (F)
Thunder: Far-Rong (M)
Rainbow: Sai-Rung (F)
Dragon: Mang-Korn (M)
Golden Dragon: Mang-Korn-Tong (M)
"Hi, how are you?": Swasdi (M or F)
Healthy: Somboon (M or F)
Moon: Chan-Tra (F)
Sun: Ah-Tith (M)
Bamboo Stick: Kin-Phai (M)
Volcano: Pu-Khoa-Fai (M)
Charming: Vi-La-Wan (F)
Little Monkey: Ling-Lek (M or F)
Little Bit: Nit-Noi (M or F)
Guard of the King: Ram-A-Sul (Pronounced Rama-Soon) (M)
Mythical Goddess: Gin-A-Ree (F)
Venus of the Orient: Nun-Taw-A-Dee (F)
Little Grasshopper: Dag-Ah-Dan (M or F)
Heart and Soul: Kwan-Jai (F)
White Monkey God: Han-U-Man (M)

Male or female, Siamese kittens are equally loveable. These four-week-old kits are from Tohpao Cattery in Westminster, California.

Spicy: Phet (M or F)
Easy-going, calm: Choi-Choi (M or F)
Mister: Nai (M)
Younger Brother: Nong-Chai (M)

MORE ABOUT PEDIGREES

The longer you're in the cat fancy and the more breeding you do, the more likely you are to develop a fascination for Siamese pedigrees—not just your own but those of other cats as well, first from breeders you've worked with and then from other breeders who have shown consistently winning Siamese.

Some American pedigrees carry British and Australian lines as well as American. These cats were imported at some point. Most of the breeders from other countries are very hospitable to United States visitors and buyers. American Siamese are sometimes sold to fanciers in other countries, especially to Japan, which has members in CFA.

When you're selling kittens, you'll need to provide a pedigree if the kittens are of breeder or show quality. It's extremely important that pedigrees be accurate and legible, preferably typewritten, and that they include the registration numbers of the first three or so generations.

A pedigree showing five generations will involve typing or writing in 32 series and dams behind the original kitten. Could you do this for your own family? It may seem excessive for your kittens at first, but later you'll recognize how helpful a full listing can be. The color of each cat should be included whether the form calls for it or not. Some breeders even go so far as to list all the other colors in each litter, helpful in some instances, but usually not known. That Lilac Point four or five generations back may account for the Lilac Point kitten that suddenly pops up in a litter of Blue Points.

You may want to get professional and have pedigrees printed up with your cattery name on vellum or you may choose just to

"When you're selling kittens, you'll need to provide a pedigree if the kittens are of breeder or show quality."

photocopy one or two originals you've bought from the registration associations, dealers at cat shows, or ordered from an ad in a cat magazine. What's important is that you provide accurate pedigrees and that you gradually become more and more knowledgable about the Siamese behind the top lines in the country; that is, if you hope to win in the show ring and to sell your kittens.

Some breeders are so taken with pedigrees that they plan their breedings almost exclusively on that basis, whereas others are more prone to study the cats in person and try to visualize what might happen from crossing them. Both can be important indications of what to expect from a breeding. A touch of intuition never seems to hurt either.

If you supply a pedigree for a pet kitten before or after neutering, you may find a three- or four-step pedigree is adequate since the cat won't be bred, and the pedigree is mainly for fun or vanity's sake. All the same, the pedigree should be accurate and neat. It does represent your cattery. You might visit those people and find they have framed the pedigree and hung it on the wall. Pet owners can be just as proud as the owners of top show cats.

Suggested Reading

The following books published by T.F.H. Publications are available at pet shops everywhere.

ATLAS OF CATS OF THE WORLD

by Dennis Kelsey-Wood
(TFH TS-127)

This book is a must for all cat fanciers—from the novice to the experienced breeder. Contains full-color photos and illustrations of every established cat breed (and many experimental varieties) as well as descriptions of wild species. Contains everything the cat lover needs to know about cats. Hardcover, 8½ x 11", 384 pages.

CAT CARE

by Dagmar Thies
(TFH KW-064)

Presents sensible, easy-to-follow recommendations about selecting and caring for cats. Illustrated with full-color photos. Hardcover, 5½ x 8", 96 pages.

ENCYCLOPEDIA OF AMERICAN CAT BREEDS

by Meredith Wilson
(TFH H-997)

An authoritative, up-to-date book that covers completely the American and Canadian breeds. A highly colorful book that is a must for cat lovers and breeders. Illustrated with full-color photos. Hardcover, 5½ x 8", 352 pages.

KITTENS

by Kay Ragland
(TFH KW-019)

For kitten and cat lovers. Presents practical information about the care of kittens. Completely illustrated with full-color photos and drawings. Hardcover, 5½ x 8", 96 pages.

SIAMESE CATS

by Ron Reagan
(TFH KW-062)

For cat lovers of all types, this book has its greatest degree of appeal to owners or potential owners of Siamese cats. Completely illustrated with full-color photos. Hardcover, 5½ x 8", 96 pages.

T.F.H. Publications is the world's largest publisher of good books about pets of all kinds.

Index

**All About
Siamese Cats
TS-129**

t.f.h.